Visiting Charles Rennie Mackintosh

VISITING CHARLES RENNIE MACKINTOSH

Roger Billcliffe

F

FRANCES LINCOLN LIMITED
PUBLISHERS

GLASGOWMACKINTOSH

Published in association with
the Mackintosh Heritage Group

Frances Lincoln Ltd
4 Torriano Mews
Torriano Avenue
London NW5
www.francesli

Copyright © Frances Lincoln Ltd 2012
Text copyright © Roger Billcliffe 2012
Photographs copyright © November 2012
except where

British Library Cataloguing in Publication data
A catalogue record for this book is available from the British Library

ISBN 978-0-7112-3285-3

9 8 7 6 5 4 3 2 1

CONTENTS

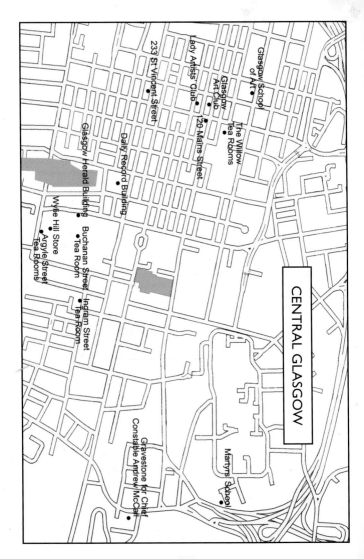

CENTRAL GLASGOW

Glasgow School of Art

The Willow Tea Rooms

Glasgow Art Club

Lady Artists' Club

120 Mains Street

233 St Vincent Street

Daily Record Building

Glasgow Herald Building

Wylie Hill Store

Buchanan Street Tea Room

Argyle Street Tea Rooms

Ingram Street Tea Room

Gravestone for Chief Constable Andrew McCall

Martyrs School

INTRODUCTION

Forty-odd years ago a small folding street map showing Mackintosh's surviving buildings in Glasgow was a great aid for me when I first visited the city. Illustrated with line drawings and short descriptive texts, it was, I am sure, equally helpful to the visitors who came to Glasgow in search of Mackintosh after seeing the 1968 centenary exhibition in Edinburgh, Darmstadt, Vienna, Zurich and London. It went out of print but has had various reincarnations, although recently they have more often taken the form of web pages than printed ones.

This small guide hopes to build on that excellent beginning and is also designed to fit in the pocket rather than on the iPad. It goes further than the original pamphlet because we now know far more about Mackintosh's work in Glasgow – and elsewhere – and it is also intended to take visitors straight to the door of these Mackintosh monuments. Hardly a day goes by without some visitor to my gallery in Glasgow asking how to get to the School of Art, or more frequently The Willow Tea Room, which is only 50 yards away but obviously not well signposted. I hope those days will now be gone.

As a bonus (because their creators very much deserve it) I have included entries on significant works by Mackintosh's contemporaries that are not easily found by the casual visitor to Glasgow. Mackintosh did not work in a vacuum, and Salmon, Gillespie, Ednie, Miller and others merit more attention – and visitors need something more easily read on the spot than the weighty, but indispensible, volumes by Gomme and Walker, and Williamson, Riches and Higgs that are devoted to the city as a whole.

Writing this guide has caused me to look again at many of Mackintosh's buildings. Since 1969 I have watched their fortunes change at the hands of politicians, planners, developers – and enthusiasts. In 1973 the Mackintosh Society was formed because of the growing threat of demolition to three of Mackintosh's buildings – Martyrs' School, Queen's Cross Church and Scotland Street School. The Ingram Street Tea Rooms had recently been dismantled and were in storage with no immediate prospect of their restoration and re-assembly. The future of the Glasgow Herald building was not secure – the newspaper wanted to relocate to more modern

7

and more flexible accommodation. The Willow Tea Rooms were a mess, hidden inside a department store. The Hill House was on the market, albeit with a very protective seller, who was not going to allow it to be pillaged. Windyhill was lived in by a reclusive Mackintosh admirer who struggled to maintain it. 78 Derngate in Northampton was the headquarters office of a wine importer and very much unloved.

Since that time there have been some wonderful success stories. And all of the buildings listed above have been 'saved', to a greater or lesser degree. In particular, the continuing restoration of the School of Art, the restoration of Mackintosh's own house by The Hunterian, the restoration of Queen's Cross Church by the Mackintosh Society, the restoration of Windyhill by successive owners and the acquisition of The Hill House by the National Trust for Scotland have secured their individual futures. Outside Glasgow, 78 Derngate has been the subject of a masterly reconstruction and development, winning awards and spawning an adjacent modern interior by John McAslan + Partners. But the outlook for some of the others is not all rosy, and current economic difficulties threaten the secure future of some of them, particularly those in public ownership in Glasgow. Mackintosh fans have to remain vigilant to ensure that we do not return to the dark days of 1970, when hardly any of Mackintosh's buildings – save, perhaps, the Glasgow School of Art under the able care of Harry Jefferson Barnes – could be guaranteed a continuing existence.

Acknowledgments

I am grateful to the Mackintosh Heritage Group for a substantial grant towards the cost of photography and other costs. Joseph Sharples and Nicky Imrie were happy to share their discoveries while working on the Mackintosh Architecture project at the University of Glasgow. We all look forward to the publication of their researches in 2014. To the owners of Mackintosh buildings who have allowed me or my photographer to intrude on their privacy, many thanks. I am also grateful to curators and publications officers of the following institutions for permission to use images from their collections: The Hunterian; Glasgow Life (Glasgow Museums); the 78 Derngate Trust.

Images used in this guide may not be reproduced without appropriate permissions from the following copyright holders:

Mackintosh and Glasgow Style collections in the UK

GLASGOW

The Hunterian
The largest collection of Mackintosh drawings and watercolours; the interiors and furniture from his own house; furniture from other commissions, notably 78 Derngate, Northampton.

Glasgow School of Art
Large collection of furniture designed primarily for the School, Windyhill or the Cranston Tea Rooms. Large group of watercolours (including other members of The Four) and architectural drawings primarily relating to the School.

Glasgow Museums
The furniture and interiors from the Ingram Street Tea Rooms; watercolours by Mackintosh and the Macdonald sisters; metalwork, posters, furniture by The Four, Talwin Morris, George Walton and many other Glasgow Style designers, a selection of which is on show (2011) in the Glasgow Style Gallery.

EDINBURGH

Scottish National Gallery of Modern Art
Watercolours and one item of furniture by Mackintosh.

National Museum of Scotland
Furniture and fittings from Dunglass Castle and other material from 34 Kingsborough Gardens and the Willow Tea Rooms. Gesso panel by Margaret Macdonald.

LONDON

Victoria & Albert Museum
Furniture, watercolours, drawings and other designs — metalwork, embroideries etc. — by The Four and other Glasgow Style designers.

RIBA Drawings Collection
Large group of drawings by Mackintosh and George Walton.

British Museum
Small group of watercolours and architectural drawings by Mackintosh.

SHEFFIELD

Graves Art Gallery
Watercolours and some furniture by Mackintosh.

BRIGHTON

Museum & Art Gallery
Furniture from Candida Cottage, Roade.

The following entries are organised thus:

- Mackintosh commissions in Glasgow, by date
- Mackintosh commissions outside Glasgow, by location
- Mackintosh's contemporaries, in and around Glasgow, alphabetically

If a site is listed as private, or not open to the public, please respect the owner's privacy and do not venture beyond the public footpath or roadway. Sites in central Glasgow and Northampton are best visited on foot or public transport and directions given are for pedestrians. Directions to other sites assume (or require) travel by car; GPS co-ordinates have been checked against Google Maps and TomTom satnav devices.

Introduction

Gravestone for
Chief Constable Andrew McCall,
Glasgow Necropolis

1888 • Charles Rennie Mackintosh
Glasgow Necropolis, 70 Cathedral Square, Glasgow G4 0UZ
Glasgow City Council

55.862097,-4.235026
NS 60482 65549
Open
0141 287 3961

Rail: High Street
Bus: 11, 19, 31, 38, 38A, 42, 56, 56A
Enter either from Cathedral Square, over bridge adjacent to south side of Cathedral, or via entrance at junction of Wishart Street and John Knox Street. In Theta Division, on hillside facing south.

Mackintosh's first public commission presumably awarded to him through connections to his father, at this time Superintendent of the City of Glasgow Police. The Celtic cross may have been requested by the client; if so it must have been a happy choice for Mackintosh who was beginning to explore Scotland's architectural history. The portrait panel is by J. Pittendrigh McGillivray; the cross was carved by Peter Smith of J. & G. Mossman. See also nearby Talwin Morris's tombstone for the Blackie family.

Wylie Hill Store

*1888–9 • John Hutchison, with James Black
details by Charles Rennie Mackintosh
20–24 Buchanan Street, Glasgow G1 3LB*

55.858406,-4.254842
NS 58992 65135
Private

Subway: St Enoch
East side of Buchanan
   Street in pedestrian
   precinct near
   junction with Argyle
   Street

The earliest building that Mackintosh is known to have worked on, albeit as a very junior draughtsman with little hint of what was to come.

140–142 Balgrayhill Road

*1890 • Charles Rennie Mackintosh
140–142 Balgrayhill Road, Glasgow G21 3AE*

55.888466, -4.230702
NS 60607 68369
Private

Adjacent to the corner of Balgrayhill
   Road at Mosesfield Street.
   Approach Balgrayhill Road from
   Hawthorn Street at Springburn
   Road.

Family tradition has it that Mackintosh was the architect for these two fairly unremarkable red sandstone villas, with his cousin as the client. If it ever existed, no typical Mackintosh detailing survives, inside or out.

Mackintosh in Glasgow

Craigie Hall

1892–3 & 1897 • Charles Rennie Mackintosh
6 Rowan Road, Glasgow G41 5BS

55.847084, -4.308228
NS 55544 63936
Private

On foot, from Paisley Road West, head south on east side of Dumbreck Road passing M8. Just after Beech Avenue enter cul de sac of Rowan Road on left.

Mackintosh assisted Keppie on two sets of additions and alterations to John Honeyman's Italianate villa of 1872. The 1892 work in the library is less overtly Mackintosh in style but his 1897 additions to the music room, with its splendid organ case, show Mackintosh in a more full-blooded manner, predicting much of the work at the Argyle Street Tea Rooms.

Mackintosh in Glasgow

Glasgow Art Club

1893 • Charles Rennie Mackintosh
187–191 Bath Street, Glasgow G2 4HU

55.864572, -4.262803
NS 58490 65783
Open Monday–Saturday, 10am–6pm
   but may vary; telephone first
0141 248 5210

Subway: Cowcaddens
Bus: First Bus 11, 18, 23, 42, 44, 51,
   57, 59
South side of Bath Street between
   Blythswood Street and Douglas
   Street

The Glasgow Art Club, having outgrown its original premises, bought two houses on Bath Street with land behind to provide new accommodation. John Keppie was a stalwart of the Club and this commission almost certainly came to Honeyman & Keppie through his contacts. Mackintosh, however, was the job architect, and surviving drawings, published in *The Bailie*, are signed by him. The bulk of the work was concentrated on an extension behind the houses to provide a Smoking Room and Gallery, but the arches in the entrance hall recall studies in Mackintosh's Italian sketchbook. The Gallery's heavy fireplaces reveal Keppie's hand, or Mackintosh working in his employer's manner, and contrast with the more typical Mackintosh detailing of ventilator covers and finger plates. The roof vault has none of Mackintosh's later use of king posts, but the frieze below it (recently rediscovered after decades of whitewashing) clearly betrays his hand in its arrangement of huge stylised thistles.

   The Gallery and other Mackintosh details survive here virtually unaltered and remain the earliest known example of the Mackintosh style.

Mackintosh in Glasgow

The Glasgow Herald (now The Lighthouse)

1893–5 • Charles Rennie Mackintosh
68–76 Mitchell Street, Glasgow G1 3LX (The Lighthouse)

55.859857, -4.255783
NS 58924 65239
Open Monday–Saturday 10.30am–
5pm; closed Sundays (but can vary
in summer, phone first)
0141 276 5360; email Information.
TheLighthouse@glasgow.gov.uk

Rail: 5 minutes' walk from either
Central Station or Queen Street
Subway: Midway between Buchanan
Street and St Enoch
Bus: First Bus 11, 18, 23, 42, 44, 51, 57,
59 (and many others along Renfield
Street/Union Street/Argyle Street)
Enter via The Lighthouse, 11 Mitchell
Lane, between Buchanan Street and
Mitchell Street

The surviving perspective at the Hunterian confirms Mackintosh's involvement in this red sandstone pile in the narrow lane of Mitchell Street. Certainly, nobody else in the office had the vocabulary that is on display here. A dominant cornice that echoes the muscularity of the details beneath it terminates four floors of production facilities and offices. Almost as in a baronial castle, two further floors project above the cornice, lit by a narrow band of window and then a series of richly ornamented dormers. And all this in a lane where such detail is almost impossible to see. At ground level the glazed bays are punched through the enormously thick wall, providing access to the print works via an internal street and to the delivery portals for distribution vehicles.

Buildings on corner sites such as this one often incorporate a tower at the junction to facilitate and emphasise the turn. Mackintosh provided such a tower here, but the adjacent elevation is on to an even narrower lane than Mitchell Street (now, 2011, the main entrance to The Lighthouse which incorporates Mackintosh's building). The tower's main function was to support a huge water tank, a fire safety precaution, at its top, decorated with stylised organic forms that enhance its outline. Its design seems to owe much to James McLaren's smaller stair turret at the High School, Stirling, which Mackintosh had drawn in a sketchbook.

A difficult building to see and worse to photograph, but it is probably

best appreciated from the top of West Nile Street, at Bath Street, where the strength of the tower can be seen silhouetted against the sky; the Mitchell Street façade is seen at its best from the upper floors of the car park on the west side of the street.

Mackintosh in Glasgow

Queen Margaret Medical College

1894–5 • Charles Rennie Mackintosh
Hamilton Drive, Glasgow, G12 8DP

55.878103, -4.286602
NS 57049 67358
Private

Subway: Hillhead. At west end of
   Hamilton Drive, near Botanic
   Gardens
Bus: First Glasgow 8, 23, 59, 66, 89,
   90, 118

At the time of writing, 2011, an isolated carcass in the wasteland, which was recently the BBC headquarters in Scotland, this building is a key member of the trio of early buildings that Mackintosh designed while still a draughtsman at Honeyman & Keppie. Together with the Herald building and Martyrs' School, it showed the development of an intellect that was to approach maturity at the Glasgow School of Art and Queen's Cross Church in 1896–9.

As at the Herald building, a tower (here in a re-entrant angle) plays an important role in articulating the junction of different parts of the building. Baronial influences are obvious, as is the repetition of decorative elements first seen at the Herald. Some gable walls, forming the perimeters of laboratories and lecture spaces, are rendered as unbroken expanses of rough masonry, a feature repeated in the east and west elevations of the School of Art in the 1896 design.

The building (with its adjacent neighbours) was incorporated into the expanded BBC headquarters and effectively hidden from view by enclosing office and studio blocks. Since the BBC departed the site for Pacific Quay it has been exposed by demolition of surrounding structures and has an uncertain future.

Mackintosh in Glasgow

Martyrs' Public School

1895–8 • Charles Rennie Mackintosh
Parson Street, Glasgow G4 0PX • Glasgow City Council

55.865394, -4.237692
NS 60081 65840
Private; open 2pm–4pm by
    appointment only
0141 553 2557

Rail: High Street
Bus: 11, 36, 37, 38, 89, 138
On foot, the pedestrian-unfriendly
    wilderness of Townhead makes
    approach difficult but from the
    main entrance to the Royal
    Infirmary, take Glebe Street
    diagonally towards Stirling Road,
    at which point a pedestrian path is
    signposted from the north side of
    Stirling Road to the school

The martyrs commemorated here, and in earlier schools near by, were four Covenanters executed in 1684.

As at the Herald building and Queen Margaret's College, the architect's perspective drawing points to Mackintosh's involvement with this design. The plan forms a stubby T with classrooms around three sides of a central hall on the ground floor, and on all four sides on the upper floors. Externally, it is dominated by the sheer mass of the red sandstone, but closer inspection reveals several typical (by 1895) Mackintosh motifs, such as the lintels above the east and west entrances which resemble details on the top floor windows at the Herald building and the organic form of the consoles either side of these doors. The patterns on the doors, in fact the whole composition of each of these entrances, are a Spook School drawing made three-dimensional. The ventilators on the roof probably have their origins somewhere in Mackintosh's Italian tour sketchbooks and the projecting eaves of each of the staircase roofs point to developments at the School of Art.

Mackintosh in Glasgow

Inside, Mackintosh's hand is immediately more obvious. The roof trusses over the hall, with their cluster of apple 'pips' on the central post, betray decorative sources from some of his earlier furniture designs and are an advance on the roof at Glasgow Art Club and look forward again to the Art School. There's also some Mackintosh games-playing here: the brackets in the hall along the wall, with their coupled projecting beams, are purely decorative and have no structural role at all. The exaggerated projecting pins in this construction are also more for show than function. Similar misleading gestures are apparent in the roofs over the staircases, where the coupled supports for the main timbers, and the double layer of cross-beams are there as much for compositional effect as structural necessity. But if one were in any doubt about Mackintosh's involvement here, it is immediately dispelled by the upward view from the floor of the hall. The vista of bulbous supports for the balcony railings, the form of the balcony doors, the subtle changes in glazing patterns on the screens and the repetitive rhythm of the arched doors with their surrounding pattern of ceramic tile all point to his control of this design.

Mackintosh in Glasgow

Mackintosh in Glasgow

Catherine Cranston

Catherine Cranston and her brother Stuart were just two of the Glasgow entrepreneurs who catered for the demand for refreshment rooms where the middle classes could meet in salubrious surroundings without being molested by the drinking classes. In fact, the first Glasgow tea room was opened by Stuart Cranston at the corner of Argyle and Queen Streets in 1875. The Cranstons were part of a teetotal dynasty whose business interests encompassed hotels, restaurants, tea rooms, tea blending and, later, cinemas. Kate (as she was known) was a visually aware lady who realised that, as all the Glasgow tea rooms provided very similar fare, she needed to offer higher standards of service and, crucially, a more exciting dining experience to attract and retain customers. She decided to employ avant-garde designers and decorators to ensure that her establishments had stylish and unusual interiors that would become talked-about and fashionable and thus continue to appeal to her clientèle.

Her early ventures were housed in rented premises, close to the business centre of Glasgow, as men were always an essential part of her business, contrary to popular belief. Ingram Street, Buchanan Street and Argyle Street housed her earliest ventures. Sadly, none of these exquisite rooms still exist *in situ*, but her one venture outside the business centre, to Sauchiehall Street with The Willow Tea Rooms, survives, albeit in a rather sorry state despite heroic efforts to restore it in 1979–80.

Kate's first tea room opened in 1878 at 114 Argyle Street, as the Crown Tea Rooms on the ground floor of Aitken's Temperance Hotel, a site that she was to redevelop over the next twenty-five years. In 1886 she opened at 205 Ingram Street, close to the Royal Exchange, then the key building for businessmen in the city. These premises were at street level of a large and relatively undistinguished block of offices with shops on the ground floor, running east from Miller Street behind the Post Office, one block from George Square. Over the following two decades she acquired almost the whole of its ground floor, opening a new room every few years. In 1896 she commissioned designs for brand new premises on several floors at 91 Buchanan Street, her first association with Mackintosh, but George Walton was really in charge of the interiors there. In 1903 she bought the tenement at 217 Sauchiehall Street and commissioned Mackintosh to transform it into her most elegant suite of rooms, The Willow Tea Rooms.

Mackintosh continued as her favoured architect in all her future extensions at Ingram Street and Argyle Street, ending his association with her in 1917 with The Dug-Out, installed in a basement immediately to the west of The Willow. The following year Miss Cranston retired from business and either closed or sold on all her tea rooms.

Shortly after they married in 1892, Kate and her husband, John Cochrane, commissioned George Walton to remodel their house in Barrhead. Walton worked for Kate Cranston on several tea rooms until he moved to London in 1897, by which time Kate was a substantial shareholder in his company. When the Cochranes moved to another house in Nitshill – Hous'hill – they asked Mackintosh to decorate several rooms, providing all of the furniture for two bedrooms, a music room and sitting room, and the hall. In 1917, after the death of her husband, Kate left Hous'hill and its furniture and settled in the North British Station Hotel in Glasgow. Hous'hill was one of Mackintosh's most important commissions, for it was there that his designs for furniture and decorations achieved maturity. Sadly, the house fell into disrepair and was eventually demolished but much of the furniture survived and individual pieces designed for it can be seen in Glasgow at Kelvingrove and The Hunterian, and at the Scottish National Gallery of Modern Art in Edinburgh and the Metropolitan Museum in New York. More substantial groups of furniture from Hous'hill are in the collections of the Musée d'Orsay in Paris and the Royal Ontario Museum, Toronto.

Buchanan Street Tea Rooms
(interiors destroyed)

1896–7 • Charles Rennie Mackintosh
91–93 Buchanan Street, Glasgow G1 3HF

55.859797, -4.254386
NS 58977 65269
Private

Subway: Buchanan Street or St Enoch
Bus: First Bus 11, 18, 23, 36, 42, 44, 51,
57, 59, 61 (and many others along
Renfield Street/Union Street/Argyle
Street)
On west side near Mitchell Lane

Only the Buchanan Street elevation remains of Kate Cranston's first custom-built tea room. It opened in 1897 on the site of an earlier tea room, the Alexandra Café, and was designed by George Washington Browne with furniture by George Walton and a decorative scheme by Walton and Mackintosh. Washington Browne's façade, variously described as François I or Northern Renaissance, was deemed elegant by local critics but *The Studio* shuddered. Certainly it was very much at odds with Walton's subtle interiors and even more so with Mackintosh's large-scale stencilled panels. His wall of statuesque female figures entwined in briar-roses in the Ladies' Lunch Room, stylised trees and peacocks in the general Lunch Room and the disturbing organic and circular shapes at the head of the stairs all announce a more public display of what had so far been a relatively private and personal 'Glasgow Style' practised by Mackintosh, MacNair and the Macdonald sisters. The Tea Room closed in 1918 on Miss Cranston's retirement and the interiors were much altered in subsequent years; nothing now remains of Walton's and Mackintosh's creations. Their loss is grievous, for our understanding of Walton, Mackintosh and Kate Cranston. For Mackintosh, these stencilled decorations were crucial in his development as an interior designer, and the ideas behind them were repeated in early designs for the School of Art, in the Ingram Street White Room in 1900, at the Vienna Secession, in Waerndorfer's Music Room, and at The Willow. Beware the lure of the 'Willow Tea Rooms' a little further up the street – twenty-first-century 'Mockintosh' taking advantage of the location.

Mackintosh in Glasgow

Argyle Street Tea Rooms (interiors destroyed)

1898 • Charles Rennie Mackintosh
108–114 Argyle Street, Glasgow G2 8BH

55.858141, -4.254445
NS 58977 65269
Private

Subway: St Enoch
Bus: First Bus 11, 18, 23, 36, 42, 44, 51,
57, 59, 61 (and many others along
Renfield Street/Union Street/Argyle
Street)
North side of Argyle Street, just east
of Buchanan Street

Miss Cranston opened her Crown Tea Room at 114 Argyle Street in 1878, but as a wedding present her husband gave her the lease to 106–114, which she redeveloped as The Crown Lunch and Tea Rooms, opening in 1898. She commissioned H. & D. Barclay to remodel the tenement, creating shops on the ground floor with each floor above given over primarily to a single room stretching the length and depth of the building. A staircase accessed from a pend behind – which is still visible – allowed gentlemen direct access to the Smoking and Billiards Rooms without having to negotiate the more public spaces entered directly from Argyle Street. The Argyle Street façade was stripped of all mouldings etc. and then harled; a fanciful roofscape of gable and dormers added a distinctly out-of-place air to the whole composition. The Tea Rooms closed in 1918. Unfortunately, all that survives of these Argyle Street Tea Rooms (apart from much of Mackintosh's furniture) is this façade – still relatively unchanged from the first floor upwards – and the turret stair behind; the interior layout with decorations by George Walton, furnished by Mackintosh, has all disappeared, including Mackintosh's 1906 basement addition, the Dutch Kitchen. In some ways the loss is more bearable than that of the nearby Buchanan Street Tea Rooms with Mackintosh's stencils, as the interiors were not particularly inspired – Walton perhaps being pre-occupied with his move to London and new work there and elsewhere – and Mackintosh's contribution was mainly restricted to moveable furniture, much of it now in several public collections in Scotland and many more across the world. His wonderful billiards tables, however, have disappeared.

These rooms were important for Mackintosh in that they provided his first opportunity to design complete room settings of furniture. The spaces undoubtedly taxed his imagination as they were predominantly barn-like, in the manner of many Glasgow tea rooms of the period which were usually furnished as refectories with long communal tables. Mackintosh tamed these vast rooms by providing furniture which sheltered its user from the larger spaces around, in the Smoking Room by grouping easy chairs around small tables for playing dominoes or cards and in the dining rooms by designing a high-backed chair which, used in groups of six or eight, gave diners a degree of privacy and intimacy denied them by the architects and by George Walton, who did little to humanise these vast spaces.

Mackintosh in Glasgow

Ingram Street Tea Rooms (interiors removed)

1900–11 • Charles Rennie Mackintosh
205–217 Ingram Street, Glasgow G1 1DQ

55.859936, -4.250507   South side of Ingram Street
NS 59246 65242   at Miller Street
Private

Miss Cranston had opened a joint venture with her brother Stuart
at 205 Ingram Street in 1886. Over the next twenty-five years she
acquired further shops to the east in this large block, also extending
south around the corner into Miller Street. From 1900 all of these
rooms were refitted by Mackintosh but none of them remains *in situ*.
He made few changes to the exterior of the building; such as they
were – windows, doors, etc. – they have all gone. The tea rooms
remained in use after Kate Cranston retired, under the ownership of
one of her former manageresses and eventually passing to Cooper's,
a chain of tea and coffee merchants with interests in grocery stores
and restaurants. In 1950 the complex was acquired by Glasgow
Corporation and the furniture removed for safe-keeping – of a not
very careful sort – while the rooms were sublet, ultimately to a
discount tourist-tat warehouse which caused considerable damage to
the remaining fittings. In 1971 a new breed of Glasgow restaurateur,
Reo Stakis, acquired adjacent premises for redevelopment as a hotel
with the option of using the Tea Rooms as bars and restaurants.
Fire regulations required so many changes, however, that planning
permission seemed unlikely to be given. Stakis's scheme was vital to
the redevelopment of an area that had fallen on hard times, and the
planning department, which had a vision of the future Merchant City,
intervened to rescue the interiors – their safe removal meant that
the Stakis scheme could go ahead.

Glasgow Museums, disgracefully, refused to take responsibility
for the fittings although requests for material from the rooms came
from as far away as the Victoria & Albert Museum and the Cooper-
Hewitt Museum in New York. Ultimately, Glasgow School of Art
stepped in with an offer to re-use the fittings in a proposed school of

architecture. In a tri-partite spirit of co-operation, the school paid for the proper recording of the rooms, the planning department paid for their removal and temporary storage and staff from the University of Glasgow lent their expertise in identifying, conserving and preserving the surviving fittings. By 1977, under a more enlightened regime, Glasgow Museums accepted responsibility for the material and began the long and difficult process of reassembling it.

Parts can be seen in displays at Kelvingrove; the White Dining Room has been completed to acclaim and is occasionally to be seen in temporary exhibitions. Work continues on the restoration and on the search for a suitable venue for the display of all of the interiors, now re-united with their furniture under the care of Glasgow Museums.

Mackintosh's work at Ingram Street encompassed his most creative years as an architect and designer. The roll-call is undeniably impressive: White Dining Room, Cloister Room, Billiards Room, 1900; the Oak Room and Billiards Room, 1906–7; Oval Room and Ladies' Rest Room, 1909–10; Chinese Room and Cloister Room, 1911.

Mackintosh in Glasgow

White Dining Room, Ingram Street Tea Rooms

1900 • Charles Rennie Mackintosh
Kelvingrove Art Gallery and Museum, Argyle Street, Glasgow G3 8AG
Glasgow Life

55.868768, -4.290075
NS 56762 66310
Open Monday–Thursday 10am–5pm;
 Friday 11am–5pm; Saturday 10am–
 5pm; Sunday 11am–5pm (may vary)
0141 276 9500; www.glasgowlife.
 org.uk/museums/our-museums/
 kelvingrove/visiting/Pages/home.aspx

Subway: Kelvinhall, but Hillhead and
 Kelvinbridge are also within walking
 distance
Bus: First Bus 9, 16, 23, 42, 62

The White Dining Room was the first of Mackintosh's tea rooms at Ingram Street for Miss Cranston. The room was painted white, with highlights in silver and silvered light fittings, while the furniture was mainly dark-stained. Customers entered and left the room via a corridor created by a wood and leaded-glass screen, which led past the cash desk and a stair to a mezzanine floor, which Mackintosh inserted to increase useable floor space. The room was dominated by two large gesso panels, *The Wassail* by Mackintosh and *The May Queen* by Margaret Macdonald. These echoed the panels of stencilling at the Buchanan Street room and were displayed at the end of 1900 in Vienna at the Secession before being installed in Glasgow.

All of the interiors from the Ingram Street Tea Rooms are now owned by Glasgow Museums. Occasionally the White Room (which was restored for the major Mackintosh exhibition of 1996) might be on display but more likely only highlights – such as the large gesso panels – will be on view in the Glasgow Style Gallery within Kelvingrove Museum. The other rooms – the Oak Room, Chinese Room, Cloister Room and so on – are still awaiting conservation. The Glasgow Style Gallery at Kelvingrove provides an excellent introduction to material by Mackintosh and The Four and other Scottish designers working in a similar manner between 1890 and 1914.

Mackintosh in Glasgow

Glasgow School of Art

1896–9, 1907–10 • Charles Rennie Mackintosh
167 Renfrew Street, Glasgow G3 6RQ
Glasgow School of Art

55.866209, -4.263747
NS 58435 65970
Access is by formal tours only; times
vary – check www.gsa.ac.uk for
current information or call 0141
353 4526
0141 353 4500

Subway: Cowcaddens
Bus: 11, 18, 23, 42, 44, 51, 57, 59
Renfrew Street, between Scott Street
and Dalhousie Street

In 1896 Glasgow School of Art launched a limited competition for premises to house a new school on Renfrew Street. Of the eleven competitors, only the drawings of the winning firm survive, those of John Honeyman & Keppie. Even before designs were submitted the competitors jointly petitioned the School to say it was impossible to provide all of the accommodation requested with the funds available, and the Governors agreed that they could indicate how much of their designs were achievable within the budget of £14,000. And so, in the first building phase, 1897–9, Mackintosh provided only the eastern half of the School, along with its central entrance and administration block. What at first may have seemed a defeat turned into a triumph. By the time the second phase was authorised Mackintosh was a partner in his firm and in full control of the job, and his later, much more personal design allowed a fuller expression of his decorative talents.

Before going inside the School, take some time to look at each of its four façades. Like no other building, it shows just how much an artist Mackintosh was. Each elevation works as an abstract composition and I defy anyone to look at a single elevation and predict the arrangement of the two adjacent façades. Whether or not this building was designed from the inside out, Mackintosh has spent a great deal of time ensuring the perfection of each of its four public faces.

It is only in recent years that the competition brief and Mackintosh's first responses to it have been available for scrutiny. The first thing to note

is that the overall layout, plans of each floor, arrangement of elevations and accommodation conform very closely to the specifications of the brief. Given that Mackintosh did not generally adhere to the niceties of a brief or budget I think we have to consider the reasons for this departure from the later norm. Two possibilities occur to me, neither exclusive of the other. Did Mackintosh help Fra Newbery, Headmaster of the School, prepare the brief? Did Mackintosh receive a considerable input from the partner in charge of the design, John Keppie? I think both are likely.

The original design for the north elevation betrays a hand other than Mackintosh's. Did Mackintosh really choose a heavy classical entablature over the studio windows, voussoired doors at the entrance and twin columns at its side. Does this not feel like Keppie? This was, after all, an important public commission, if not particularly remunerative, and Keppie would undoubtedly have kept an eye on it. And where did these huge windows come from? Certainly not Mackintosh's earlier work; but their form and dimensions are almost spelt out in the brief. And so are the depths of each studio, the need for them to be interconnected and the possibility to open walls to allow adjacent rooms to function as one. What is undeniably Mackintosh's input to this north elevation are the various pieces of decorative sculpture, finials and decorated roof vents, and the detailed arrangement of the entrance and Headmaster's Room above. Almost all of the decorative elements were to disappear (along with the columns, voussoirs and entablature) as the north elevation was stripped down to save money. And this is what drove the utilitarian appearance of the School, not a design aesthetic.

Mackintosh was at his best and happiest when able to incorporate some form of decoration in his architectural work – 'living fancy' as Sedding called it – but it was often removed to save costs. His designs for A House for an Art Lover show how he would ideally have incorporated exterior sculpture and internal stencils and gesso work. So the simple, rough interiors of the School of Art are a product of client parsimony rather than design aesthetic. That Mackintosh could make so much of so little merely reinforces his own versatility and originality.

The School is approached through its main entrance in the centre of the asymmetrical façade to Renfrew Street (this asymmetry was evident in even the earliest surviving designs for the School). It shows Mackintosh's eclecticism, with its borrowings from English vernacular in the projecting eastern bay, inspired by a drawing of a house in Bridport in one of his sketchbooks. The window above the door, lighting the Headmaster's Room, is borrowed from James McLaren, and is repeated on the east elevation. Originally the area between the retaining wall and the School was open, like a moat, reinforcing its castle-like appearance. Subsidiary doors on the east and (later) west elevations give access

Mackintosh in Glasgow

to the basement level, where the sculpture and metal-working studios were arranged so that their noise was isolated from the rest of the building and their messy materials could be supplied direct from the street without intruding on the upper floors.

The east door led almost directly to the Living Animal Studio and larger specimens (an elephant and camel are recorded) were brought to it from Hengler's Circus on Sauchiehall Street. The east elevation is effectively a Scottish castle, with references to several of the castles Mackintosh had earlier recorded in his sketchbooks, notably Maybole, the source for the corbel beneath the oriel tower that originally housed a tiny staircase giving access to a top-lit mezzanine studio above the original Board Room, the latter identified by its shallow bay windows on the left, south, side of this elevation.

The massive south elevation, because of the slope of the site the largest of all, is almost completely encased in harling, punctured by a few windows at higher levels and relieved only by the occasional use of a piece of dressed stone, especially to the west of the centre block added in 1907–10. The brief limited the form and number of windows here, which Mackintosh has put to good effect with a design that takes the modernisation of Scottish vernacular, seen on the east elevation, to further heights.

The internal centrepiece of this first phase is the Museum on the first floor. Its walls were originally rendered with the simple (and undoubtedly inexpensive) panelling which lined the corridors and studios and was here believed to have been stained green. The space is dominated by a trussed roof and is top-lit. Mackintosh's famous games-playing is evident here in the columns around the staircase, which appear to support the massive roof trusses. As in the later Library, however, they offer little support to the main beams, which are firmly anchored in the masonry of the north and south walls where all the weight of the roof is taken. In a set of drawings submitted for Dean of Guild Court permission, Mackintosh shows a painted or low relief frieze of figures in the space above the panelling, roughly 2m high. Reminiscent of the stencilling at the Buchanan Street Tea Rooms – although (in this drawing, at least) not so stylised – the frieze would have gone some way to balance the austerity of the fitting out of the School.

The studios, as specified by Newbery, are wonderful spaces in which to paint – simple, without distractions and beautifully lit. The mezzanine floors are additions from the 1960s. At the east end of the first floor corridor the original Board Room houses a very fine fireplace, perhaps the largest fireplace Mackintosh designed – and evidence of the Board's reluctance to skimp on its own accommodation.

Work began on the second phase of the School of Art in 1907. As a partner in his firm Mackintosh now had sole control over the design and there would have been no input from Keppie. This second phase provided the accommodation west of the entrance block; the north and south elevations broadly followed the original design but the west elevation, to Scott Street, was completely redesigned. Other additions and alterations included a third storey, sitting on top of the main studios but set back

Mackintosh in Glasgow

from the north elevation; two extra staircases within the re-entrant angle of the east and west blocks; and the infilling of the area at basement level on the north elevation to provide extra studio space.

The southern part of the west elevation, containing a lecture theatre, architecture studios, library, library store and Composition Room, stacked one above the other, is Mackintosh's most dynamic design. At basement level the School is entered through a dramatic composition of a door, belying its relative insignificance as an entrance to the School. Its form is a counterpoint of recession and projection surmounted by a stepped hood that is reminiscent of some of the drawings of gravestones in Mackintosh's sketchbooks. A niched platform above the deeply recessed door seems to be designed for a piece of sculpture, which Mackintosh originally intended to use to great effect elsewhere on this elevation. Above the door, at ground floor level, runs a row of six bay windows lighting the architecture studios; their dressed stone forms a foil to the rough stone of the gable wall of the first floor studio above. These bays, a continuation of the theme for the bay seen east of the entrance door, are continued upwards in the southern half of this

elevation – in glass to light the library and its store and then in masonry at second floor level to accentuate the soaring height of the building. These windows are detailed with a surrounding stone moulding, projecting and receding at times like those on the basement door. Each window is flanked by a drum of stone, often mistaken for part of the overall abstract composition of the façade but in fact intended by Mackintosh to be carved into huge columnar figures. This reflects Mackintosh's belief in the importance of sculptural ornament; had they ever been executed the perception of this elevation as a masterpiece of twentieth-century Modernism might well have been tested.

The south elevation of this block repeats many of the same features – but almost as a negative rendition of its western counterpart. The architecture studio windows are set within the thickness of the wall, as are the lower windows to the library. The central windows, however, continue Mackintosh's games-playing counterpoint theme, here being encased in dressed stone in contrast to the harling around them, while the upper window, lighting the studio, is glazed on three sides and sits within a wide niche.

Inside, the studios in the west phase of the School broadly follow the pattern established by 1899, albeit with a more sophisticated eye and a greater attention to detail. The library, however, is one room that demands particular attention, its multi-layered composition revealing fascinating detail. Perhaps this is a metaphor for the Tree of Knowledge, its central posts and trailing beams echoing a copse of young trees, with the colour on the balusters representing blossom. Structurally, the floor and main columns are supported on beams running east–west but the columns do not actually support the ceiling and floor above – the library store – which is suspended from more beams running above the store that support also the Composition Room above. More Mackintosh games.

The Composition Room, on the second floor, is overtly Japanese in its coupled beams and columns supporting the roof – one of the most serene spaces in the School. This second floor has an ingenious arrangement to ensure circulation from east to west around the impenetrable mass of masonry that is the Headmaster's Studio. Although Mackintosh was able to add a lightweight second floor to the roof of the original section of the School he was unable to extend it south to meet the boundary wall – as happened in the 1907 extension – because this would have obliterated

the roof lights in the first floor's east corridor, its only source of daylight. On the new western section of the school he was able to build out to the south wall and provided a corridor – a loggia, it is called on his plans – which looks out over the city and projects beyond the line of the centre block's Headmaster's Studio. To connect to the second floor corridor on the eastern half of the School – set back beyond the southern line of that studio – Mackintosh provided a glazed walkway that appears to float above the museum roof but is in fact supported on a series of brackets attached to the south wall of the Headmaster's Studio. Nicknamed 'The Hen Run' by generations of students it provides an airy (but very hot on a sunny day) solution to an apparently intractable problem.

Glasgow School of Art requires a careful study of its layers of detail. The apparent simplicity of the design hides a multi-faceted response to Newbery's brief, which laid out the basic plan of the School. It shows, in the first phase, Mackintosh responding to the arduous demands of a client reducing his scope by cutting his budget; and later the Mackintosh who would persist in ignoring a client's demand for economy and then provide him with a world-class building.

Queen's Cross Church

1897–9 • Charles Rennie Mackintosh
870 Garscube Road, Glasgow G20 7EL
The Charles Rennie Mackintosh Society

55.8803, -4.272169
NS 57976 67572
March–October: Open Monday,
    Wednesday and Friday 10am–5pm.
    Guided tours 11am and 2.30pm.
    Adults £4, Concessions £2, Children
    free. Free entry on Wednesday
    afternoons after 1pm.
November–March: Open Monday,
    Wednesday and Friday 10am–4pm.
    Guided tours 11am.
0141 946 6600; www.crmsociety.com/
    Mackintoshchurch.aspx for revisions
    to opening times etc.

Rail: Central or Queen Street Station
    then bus as below
Subway: St George's Cross then
    15-minute walk through Cromwell
    Street into Maryhill Road, north-
    west to junction of Garscube Road
Bus: 40, 61 from Hope Street at
    Central Station

Surprisingly, it was John Keppie who obtained this commission, not John Honeyman, who was well known as a church architect. As Keppie's assistant, Mackintosh developed the job – indeed, took it over – while working at the same time on Glasgow School of Art.

Mackintosh adopted a Free Gothic style for the church: superficially its detailing and massing suggest a fifteenth-century Decorated style, but closer inspection reveals a much more modern and ingenious plan, and decorative details which show an idiosyncratically inventive Mackintosh. The site is very tight and was originally adjacent to high tenements on Garscube Road and Maryhill Road. Mackintosh maximised the space available for the congregation to worship by providing virtually a single interior space that takes up almost the entire site except for a church hall to the rear of the plot. Externally, this simplicity is concealed by a lively elevation to Garscube Road, liturgically the north elevation but actually facing south. The adjoining façade to Springbank Street consists primarily of a large traceried

window lighting the chancel of the church. At their junction Mackintosh inserted a short tapering tower with attached octagonal stair tower. In the typical approach to the church, from the north-west Maryhill Road, the tower dominates the design; its source is the tower of Merriott Church in Somerset, which Mackintosh had sketched in 1895. The door on the south side of this tower leads to a porch and then to a passage aisle running the full length of the south side of the church, terminating in a second, similar, porch and door at the south-east corner of the church. From each of these porches a stair ascends to the galleries; and from the passage aisle two further aisles cross the church, giving access across the rows of pews to the north side of the church and the church hall.

The main body of the church is one large space, seating 559, under a timber barrel-vaulted roof spanned by steel tie-beams, unashamedly exposed, although Dean of Guild drawings suggest these were once intended to be timber framed.

Mackintosh in Glasgow

Seen from the south-east the church appears to present a traditional cruciform plan. In reality, the two 'transept' bays are only visual projections and do not reflect an internal crossing, their windows at ground level lighting the passage aisle and those above the south gallery. To the east of them Mackintosh has enclosed the passage aisle in a low structure, set back from the building line and with a lower roof, to increase the articulation of this elevation and forcing him to introduce a flying buttress to take some of the thrust of the internal tie-beams.

Internally, the church is restrained, with dark-stained wooden panelling and pews. On the front of the galleries pendant panels predict similar detailing at the School of Art, and in the hall a fine trussed roof reiterates Mackintosh's control of the design.

The church may well have a radical plan and Mackintosh's by-now common games-playing in its layout, but it is the detailing that confirms Queen's Cross Church as a true Mackintosh design. Whether or not the overall style – fifteenth- and sixteenth-century Gothic – was specified by the client or chosen by Mackintosh (it would not have been a natural language for Keppie), it gave Mackintosh countless opportunities to express his love and mastery of architectural ornament properly incorporated into a modern design. That is not to say this is a Gaudí fantasy, but Mackintosh uses both architectural detailing and sculptural ornament to enliven a building beset by prosaic tenements – now almost all demolished and never as fanciful as those shown in Mackintosh's perspective drawing. The south elevation has carved capitals, traceried windows, sculptural niches, carvings of birds, flowers and leaves alongside sinuous drip mouldings and expressive door casings and lintels on the secondary doors to the vestry and hall. Inside, the detailing of the pulpit, communion table and alms dishes reflects the stone detailing of capitals, piscina and roof trusses. Imagine what the first phase of the School of Art might have looked like had Mackintosh's imagination been allowed to run off with the client's purse.

Mackintosh in Glasgow

Westdel (interiors removed)

1898 • Charles Rennie Mackintosh
2 Queen's Place, Glasgow G12 9DQ

55.876867, -4.3004340
NS 56180 67249
Private

Subway: Hillhead
From Byres Road, take Dowanside
road and turn right on Crown Road
North. First right into Queen's
Place

This was an important commission for Mackintosh. It came from the Glasgow publisher James MacLehose who asked Mackintosh (not Honeyman & Keppie) to remodel an attic bedroom. Mackintosh created his first white space, with furniture and fittings painted white and a stencilled pattern of stylised plants as a frieze. The house was given to Glasgow University before 1950 and used as a faculty house. The interiors have been removed and are now in the collection at The Hunterian.

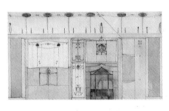

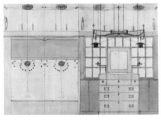

233 St Vincent Street

1898–9 • Charles Rennie Mackintosh
233 St Vincent Street, Glasgow G2 5QY

55.862114, -4.2637411
NS 58421 65532
Private

Rail: Central Station, Queen Street
   Station, Charing Cross
Subway: Buchanan Street
Bus: First Bus 5, 9, 11, 12, 20, 38, 38A,
   40, 40A, 41, 44, 57, 57A
On south side of St Vincent Street
   between Blythswood and Douglas
   Streets

The major part of this commission for Honeyman & Keppie was the provision of rooms at the rear of the building for which Mackintosh designed a beamed roof similar to those in the halls at Queen's Cross and Ruchill Church Halls, although somewhat smaller. Other Mackintosh details, such as doors and decorative niches, were removed in a 1980s redevelopment but elements from the hall were incorporated in the rebuild of the block, carried out by Keppie Design.

Ruchill Street Free Church Halls

1898–9 • Charles Rennie Mackintosh
15 Shakespeare Street, Glasgow G20 8TH
Ruchill Kelvinside Parish Church, Church of Scotland

55.886769, -4.283702
NS 57286 68315
Private
Opening times vary, telephone
    first (0141 946 0466) or email
    enquiries@ruchillparish.org.uk

Bus: 40, 61
Shakespeare Street, north of Maryhill
    Road (opposite McDonalds)

The halls were built before the adjoining church as mission halls for
Westbourne Free Church. The commission for the church in 1903 went
to Neil Duff.

The interiors of the halls are typical for the date, being primarily
panelled in dark stained wood under a timber roof and with glazed
panels in doors, all reminiscent of Queen's Cross Church hall and the
School of Art. It is the exterior, the elevation to Shakespeare Street,
that is of particular interest. Here is Mackintosh the Free Style architect,
with a composition that introduces four different window forms, an
elaborate doorcase and modern 'medieval' tracery, alongside niches
for (unprovided) sculpture and prominent rainwater heads, all in the
frontage of a relatively minor and obscure church hall. Can you see the
face in the right-hand window block?

Lantern and Finial at Pettigrew & Stephens Department Store

1899 • Charles Rennie Mackintosh
The Hunterian, University of Glasgow,
82 Hillhead Street, Glasgow G12 8QQ
University of Glasgow

55.873006, -4.2886752
NS 56901 66795
Open 9.30am–5.00pm, Monday to
   Saturday. Admission free to Art
   Gallery, Mackintosh House £3/£2
0141 330 5431

Subway: Hillhead or Kelvinbridge
Bus: First Buses 44, 44A

Honeyman & Keppie were commissioned by Messrs Pettigrew and Stephens to design a new warehouse/department store – in the western part of the block bounded by Sauchiehall Street, West Campbell Street and Bath Street. It was demolished in 1968/9. Although Mackintosh does not seem to have been seriously involved with the design, the dome over the building at the corner of Sauchiehall Street and West Campbell Street bears strong resemblance to his design for a Chapter House (1891–2). The lantern atop the dome, originally virtually invisible from the ground, was preserved during the building's demolition and is now on display in the courtyard of The Hunterian. Its iron finial and other decorative details confirm the hand of Mackintosh.

Mackintosh in Glasgow

Interiors at 120 Mains Street
(now Blythswood Street)

1900 • Charles Rennie Mackintosh
120 Blythswood Street, Glasgow G2 4EA
(interiors now at The Hunterian)

55.864391, -4.261901
NS 5854 6576
Private

Subway: Cowcaddens
Bus: 11, 18, 23, 42, 44, 51, 57 and 59
East side of Blythswood Street at
    junction with Bath Street

Although Mackintosh only lived here from 1900 to 1906 (and took away the features he had designed when he moved to Florentine Terrace) it is interesting to see where Mackintosh stayed after his marriage to Margaret Macdonald in 1900 and how ideally he was situated. Theirs was the first floor flat in this tenement at the corner of Mains Street (now renamed Blythswood Street) and Bath Street. From here, in less than five minutes, he could walk to his office, to the School of Art, to the Lady Artists' Club, to Glasgow Art Club (although he was never a member), to The Willow Tea Rooms around the corner in Sauchiehall Street. Nothing remains in the flat, the only record of Mackintosh having lived here being the current owner's nameplate – Mackintosh House.

Mackintosh in Glasgow

Daily Record Building

1901 • Charles Rennie Mackintosh
20–28 Renfield Lane, Glasgow G2 5AR

55.861116, -4.257696
NS 58788 65411
Private, although part of the ground
    floor is used as a pub and café

Rail: Central Station.
Subway: Buchanan Street
Bus: First Bus 12, 19, 29, 38, 45, 45C,
    56, 138
From Central Station, north up Hope
    Street and first right into Renfield
    Lane

Hidden away between Renfield Lane and St Vincent Lane is Mackintosh's second newspaper printing works in Glasgow. The Renfield Lane elevation is the most important, with a six-storey block of offices west of a four-storey printing works. The ground floor is in sandstone, articulated by bold arches with a central bank of oriel windows over a door with a massive keystone that is the forebear of the west door at Glasgow School of Art. The upper floors are of glazed brick, the lower blue and higher white, the latter often found in these narrow

lanes, with occasional stone dressings to windows. A projecting cornice over the offices hides a further row of dormer windows, all in stone and reminiscent of the top floor at the Herald building. Between the bays Mackintosh has inserted projecting tiled bricks which form the tree trunks for a triangular canopy of red bricks at the upper floor, a predecessor of the stencilled decoration in the hall at 78 Derngate, Northampton. The elevation to St Vincent Lane is along the same lines but much simpler, although it does repeat the tall glazed-brick trees.

34 Kingsborough Gardens

1901–2 • Charles Rennie Mackintosh
34 Kingsborough Gardens, Glasgow G12 9NJ

55.87903, -4.304237
NS 55963 67487 NS 55948 67489
Private

Little remains of the internal alterations Mackintosh made to this house (originally 14 Kingsborough Gardens by D.W. Sturrock) for the aunt (by marriage) of Fra Newbery, Headmaster of Glasgow School of Art. At the time its drawing room was Mackintosh's most ambitious and elaborate domestic interior composition. Most of its constituent parts are now destroyed or scattered to public and private collections but the fireplace remains *in situ*.

The House for an Art Lover

1901 & 1989–96 • Charles Rennie Mackintosh
Bellahouston Park, 10 Dumbreck Road, Glasgow G41 5BW
House for an Art Lover Ltd

55.847373, -4.313947
Entrance for cars 55.846759,
    -4.310417
NS 55227 63996
Opening hours vary: telephone
    first (0141 353 4770) or email
    enquiries@houseforanartlover.
    co.uk or check website www.
    houseforanartlover.co.uk

In Bellahouston Park; enter from
    Dumbreck Road

Mackintosh probably learned of the competition to design a House for an Art Lover (Haus eines Kunstfreundes) while he and Margaret Macdonald were in Vienna for the 8th exhibition of the Vienna Secession in December 1900. The final date for entries was close and on his return to Glasgow Mackintosh seems to have hurriedly pulled together a design, merging existing interiors from the concurrent Windyhill with more grandiose exteriors that took his modern Scottish vernacular style to new heights. He was unplaced in the competition, disqualified because he did not provide the requisite numbers and types of drawing specified in the brief. As a consolation, the judges awarded him a special prize for the quality of his drawings and the competition sponsor, the publisher Alex Koch, included them among a group of portfolios he published to mark the judging of the competition, where no outright winner was declared. It is not clear whether Koch ever intended to build any of the entries and, although his entry earned him respect from his European peers, Mackintosh's powerful design languished unbuilt.

In the late 1980s Graham Roxburgh, a Glasgow engineer who then lived in Craigie Hall where Mackintosh had made additions in the 1890s, conceived a scheme to bring the design to life. It was a bold plan, not least because Mackintosh had only left fourteen drawings relevant to the building. All of the craftsmen who were used to working with Mackintosh

– sculptors, masons, decorators and furniture makers – were long out of business. Roxburgh had the drive, contacts and enthusiasm to see the project through, however, and despite many difficulties – practical and financial – the house was eventually completed in 1996.

The building is certainly impressive – its scale alone demands attention and shows Mackintosh's ingenuity and imagination. But this is a huge building and one must ask whether it would have been buildable for the sums outlined in the competition, and whether any Scottish client would have, or could have, commissioned such a house. There is no doubt that the design would have evolved had Mackintosh ever had the opportunity to build it, as did all of his major buildings, but even as a slavish rendering of a handful of drawings the structure commands respect. The massing and skilful integration of a lot of sculpture has been well interpreted by the building's architect, Andy MacMillan, but the interior is less happy. Much of the decoration is not sensitively handled and there is a hard-edged quality to it that Mackintosh would not have imposed. And surely Mackintosh would have developed some themes and suppressed others?

Do these questions now matter? The building exists; it has found a purpose, forged for itself a successful and valid life, making a contribution to its community and offering services and amenities in short supply in the area. It has made a relatively obscure design come to life. Whether that design should have stayed on the shelf is now a purely academic talking point. No doubt some of its visitors are convinced it is the real thing, a Mackintosh design overseen by its creator. It isn't, but viewed as a work in progress the building still has insights to offer us.

Mackintosh in Glasgow

The Willow Tea Rooms and The Dug-Out

1903 & 1916 • Charles Rennie Mackintosh
217 Sauchiehall Street, Glasgow G2 3EX

55.865096, -4.2610753
NS 58599 65858
Open Monday–Saturday, 9am–5.30pm;
 Sundays and Bank Holidays 11am–
 5pm. Tea Room hours 9am–5pm;
 Sundays and Bank Holidays
 11am–5pm.

Subway: Cowcaddens
Bus: 11, 18, 23, 42, 44, 51, 57, 59
Sauchiehall Street, between West
 Campbell Street and Blythswood
 Street

Sauchiehall means 'alley of the willows' and Kate Cranston and Mackintosh seized on this theme for the new tea room they built here. Kate acquired numbers 215 and 217, originally tenements sharing a common stair (all of the tenement stairs have now been removed in this block). Mackintosh's remodelling enclosed the original common staircase and provided another stair at the rear of the building for the use of tenants at 215.

The Willow Tea Rooms thus became a single unit and was the only tea room where Mackintosh was able to exercise total control over both architectural and decorative elements. Although hampered by the adjacent structures to east and west he was able to design a new street elevation and a new elevation to the lane at the back. The extension at the rear was certainly reworked by him but a structure may have existed when Kate acquired the property. There were four main dining rooms, a billiards and smoking room on the second floor and kitchens in the basement. In 1917 Mackintosh created another room, the Dug-Out, in the basement of the shop to the west, entered from the ground floor saloon of The Willow. The door to The Willow from the street led to the main staircase and the cash desk. To the right was entry to the Front and Rear Saloons; the former bright with white paint and dark ladderback chairs, arranged in tables of four over a geometric-patterned carpet; the latter more atmospheric, darker with a low ceiling created by the mezzanine gallery above and stencilled panels in muted colours on the walls. Both rooms had elaborate fireplaces and leaded glass panels were used extensively for decoration. The main stair led first to the Gallery Tea Room at the back of the building, with similar

Mackintosh in Glasgow

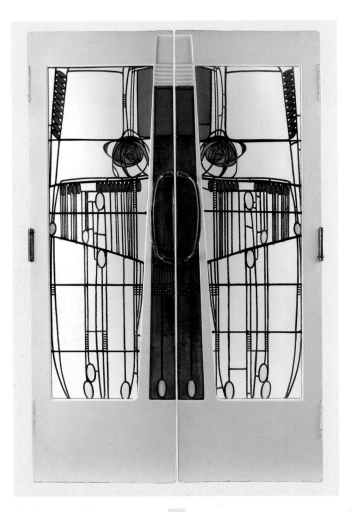

furniture as the Rear Saloon beneath it but bathed in natural light from the extensive glazed roof. Again, stencilled panels, wrought-iron screens and leaded glass complemented the elegant fireplace on the south wall.

Customers who continued up the stair beyond the mezzanine reached the jewel-like core of The Willow, the Room de Luxe, or Ladies Room as it was called on Mackintosh's drawings for its furniture. Here the tone changed abruptly, abandoning the geometric feel of the lower floors with their boxy furniture and dark/light counterpoints in favour of curves and a theme of silver and purple. The shallow curve of the full-width bay window was echoed at 90° in the vaulted ceiling. The silver painted furniture was upholstered in pink-purple velvet that also covered the banquettes ranged around the walls. Low chairs faced the banquettes and were arranged around the three circular tables in the bay window. In the centre of the room, two tables, carefully placed within the geometric pattern of the carpet, were each surrounded by four high-backed chairs; within an already intimate space Mackintosh created two islands of privacy with these tall chairs, their tops decorated with a pattern of nine squares of coloured glass. The spiritual intensity of this room was heightened by the addition of four set-pieces, each of them a powerful design in its own right: leaded-glass doors at the entrance; a gesso panel made by Margaret Macdonald; a fireplace opposite this with an elaborate leaded-glass panel above it; and, suspended from the ceiling, a large chandelier of glass globes, hanging at different heights and lit by electricity. The main staircase carried on to a Billiards Room and Gentlemen's Smoking Room above, where the geometric themes of the Rear Saloon were repeated in a dark decorative scheme befitting its masculine use.

When she retired in 1918 Miss Cranston sold The Willow and it was renamed The Kensington – after the name of the terrace in which it was located. It was not much altered but in 1927 it closed and its furniture was sold at auction. One young architect was able to buy eight chairs from the Room de Luxe for an average of two shillings and sixpence (12p) each, about £5 today. Daly's, the fashion store to the east of The Willow, acquired it and began to make substantial changes. Most of the east party-wall on the ground floor was demolished and many of the original fittings were removed or hidden. The Room de Luxe remained relatively intact, under a coat of white paint, but the ground floor windows and door were removed. In the late 1970s Daly's moved to a new block on Sauchiehall Street and their original building was acquired by a pension

Mackintosh in Glasgow

fund. Planning permission for redevelopment of the block imposed strict conditions, including the separation of 217 from the rest of the block, thus recreating the original unit that Mackintosh had made. Mackintosh's firm, now Keppie Henderson, was appointed to restore the building to as near its 1903 condition as possible. Much that was original was uncovered and where necessary sympathetic replicas were installed. Two triumphs were the reinstatement of the interiors, including mezzanine, of the rear building and of the windows and door to Sauchiehall Street.

All the new building required was a sympathetic tenant. It did not get one. The jeweller/gift shop on the ground floor has not responded to the ethos of Mackintosh's great design, nor to the hard work of the building's restorers in 1979–80, covering up much of the restoration (and some original items) with unsympathetic shop fittings. Its stock covers the whole gamut of Mockintosh. The Room de Luxe has lost its charm – and much of its serenity – through poor detailing of the replacement furniture and its arrangement, but twenty-first-century rents probably demand even more of a return on each chair than did Kate Cranston of her architect. Still, getting it right and re-creating the Mackintosh experience in its entirety might just provide that necessary premium.

THE DUG-OUT

It may seem odd to us now that Miss Cranston should capitalise on what is today seen as one of the horrors of the First World War by opening a tea room with the name Dug-Out. She was doubtless taking advantage of the patriotic spirit that still prevailed at the end of 1916 and Mackintosh certainly lived up to his reputation of providing a striking design, with black-painted walls and ceilings off-set by brightly coloured furniture and wall paintings.

Although entered from The Willow, the new tea room was actually situated in the basement of the building to the west, now Sainsbury's. The style that Mackintosh had perfected at 78 Derngate in Northampton made its only appearance in Scotland in this basement cavern. Stencilled decoration was similar to that in the hall at Derngate, linear tapes on walls and ceiling echoed Derngate's guest bedroom and lattice patterns dominated furniture, screens and doors. Like its namesakes in the French battlefields, nothing remains of it today, except for a few pieces of furniture, some of which are in the collection at the GSA.

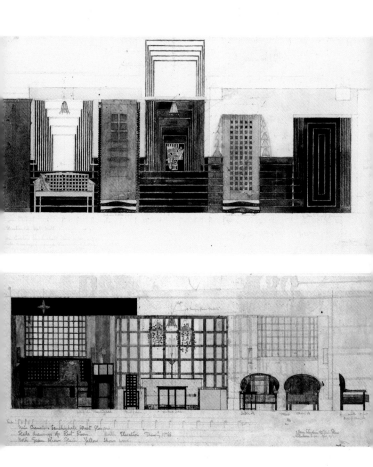

Mackintosh in Glasgow

Scotland Street School

1903–6 • Charles Rennie Mackintosh
225 Scotland Street, Glasgow G5 8QB
Glasgow Life (Scotland Street School Museum)

55.849771, -4.2737138
NS 57752 64179
Open Tuesday–Saturday, 10am–5pm;
   Sunday 11am–5pm
0141 287 0500

Subway: Shields Road
Bus: First Bus 88, 90

Mackintosh in geometric mode. The plan is regulation school board, with drill hall on the ground floor, classrooms above, separate entrances and staircases for girls and boys with adjacent cloakrooms, but the beauty of this school is in the details and the way Mackintosh interpreted the plan.

The north elevation is the most expressive, dominated by the two cylindrical staircase towers – columns of glass with stone mullions which terminate in extended capitals beneath a sinuous transom. These same capitals are repeated at the same height in a bank of masonry either side of the columns of glass, but here they are more elaborate with a varying arrangement which recalls the pendants on the gallery panels at Queen's Cross Church, the classical detailing of the School of Art Board Room and foreshadows the detailing of the Library pendants at the Art School. Above the transom the columns are fluted before they terminate under a conical slate roof. The school may be relatively simple but Mackintosh has not forsaken the sculptural detail that marks all of his public buildings. It appears again at ground level in the entrance doors beneath the glass towers and in the delightful miniature entrance for infants in the centre of the façade.

Either side of the towers (which owe more than a nod to the towers at Falkland Palace that Mackintosh had drawn several years before) the cloakrooms are set in a receding tier and appear to cascade down the façade, giving a fluidity which contrasts with the classroom block's solidity. A similar movement is created by the curves of the perimeter wall at Scotland Street but elsewhere geometric formality is the norm,

except in the janitor's house, which is reminiscent of English Arts and Crafts architecture, particularly Voysey.

This geometry is most apparent on the south elevation, with its banks of classroom windows that typify so many Glasgow schools of the period. Mackintosh articulated the eighteen-bay façade by concentrating decorative elements in the outermost and two central bays. The end bays are given weight through fluted architraves around each window, the lower two of which have scalloped mouldings that project from the building plane. Between the windows of each floor Mackintosh introduced further sculptural panels, a Glasgow Style motif between ground and first floor and more fluted columns with overlapping triangles of stone between first and second floors. The central bays project slightly, repeating the fluted architraves, but the highlight is the composition around the two second-floor windows. Several of the motifs here correspond to similar features in Mackintosh's contemporary designs for furniture

Mackintosh in Glasgow

(or vice versa) such as the boss covered with overlapping triangles of stone, the scalloped fluting at either side of the bays and the chequer board of squares at the top, inlaid with green tiles and overlaid with more triangles. Is this another stylised Tree of Knowledge?

Coloured tiles are also used inside the school, particularly in the drill hall and on the staircases, whose stairs form doglegs within the twin towers, and do not follow the curve of the outer walls.

There is much here that presages the west front of Glasgow School of Art and looks even further forward to the late rooms at Ingram Street (the Chinese Room and second Cloister Room) and the hall parlour at 78 Derngate, Northampton. Even in a relatively straightforward commission for a Board school, Mackintosh shows how careful detailing and imaginative design can lift even the most mundane of buildings.

The school lost its catchment area forty years ago and its continuing existence was uncertain for many years before Glasgow Museums took it over as a museum of education. Unfortunately, like other Mackintosh projects associated with Glasgow Life (such as Martyrs' School and the Ingram Street Tea Rooms) there no longer seems to be the commitment to a secure future and at the time of writing, 2011, there are growing concerns over its condition and prospects.

6 Florentine Terrace

1906 • Charles Rennie Mackintosh
The Hunterian, University of Glasgow,
82 Hillhead Street, Glasgow G12 8QQ
University of Glasgow

55.873006, -4.2886752
NS 56901 66795
Open Monday–Saturday 9.30am–5pm;
   admission free to Art Gallery,
   Mackintosh House £3/£2
0141 330 5431

Subway: Hillhead or Kelvinbridge
Bus: First buses 44, 44A
Parking: Metered

In 1906 the Mackintoshes moved from their flat in Mains Street to a house in Hillhead. 6 Florentine Terrace (later re-numbered as 78 Southpark Avenue) was at the southern end of a terrace, with views over Wellington Church and Gilbert Scott's University of Glasgow. It was an unexceptional mid-Victorian building, but Mackintosh was to transform its three floors with fittings he brought from Mains Street and some clever alterations. After the Mackintoshes left Glasgow they sold the house and much of its furniture to William Davidson, who was finding Windyhill too big for him. After his death in 1945 the house was bought by the University of Glasgow; its furniture was presented to the University by Davidson's family. For the next twenty years it served as a faculty house for the University's growing professoriate. It would be uplifting to think that the University bought the house to preserve it but the truth is that the property was one of many in Hillhead that were acquired by the University with an eye on post-war expansion. Hillhead had been the site of much uncharted coal mining in the eighteenth and nineteenth centuries and subsidence threatened much of the area. As the end house in the terrace number 78 was particularly at risk and by the early 1960s its problems were manifest. The interiors were photographed, measured and the important parts removed into storage; demolition followed with the promise of reconstruction in the proposed new art gallery, designed by Whitfield Partners, to be constructed one block west on Hillhead Street. The University was spared the ignominy of

Mackintosh in Glasgow

demolishing the house simply to create space for the deadly dull refectory building which later occupied its site. Andrew McLaren Young, in charge of the University's art collections (including the vast archive of Mackintosh material received in 1947), was determined that criticism of the University for demolishing the house should be overturned. His brief to architect William Whitfield included a full reconstruction of the house's interiors in the Library and the Hunterian complex proposed for Hillhead Street. Whitfield's original plan was to present

the individual rooms on one floor in a traditional museum arrangement. This would have ignored Mackintosh's important additions to the fabric of the house; eventually the job architect, Andrew 'Red' Mason (who went on to complete a masterly restoration of Hawksmoor's Christ Church, Spitalfields) and the author – appointed to the Hunterian in 1969 – devised the adopted solution where the house's interiors were reconstructed almost exactly as Mackintosh left them, their orientation and layout exactly replicating his design. The house may look odd to visitors to Whitfield's gallery, a Victorian composition set into the bush-hammered walls of a 1960s design, but it sits where it is to ensure that the rooms are lit just as they were in 1906 and that the views from the windows that Mackintosh inserted are pretty much the same today as they were then. Because of this the front door is lifted above street level, and this usually incites comment, but access to the house was always envisaged as being from inside the Gallery, never from the street.

The ground floor dining room followed much the same format as at 120 Mains Street – indeed Mackintosh brought the fireplace and doors from his flat. The walls are covered in dark wallpaper, a form of kraft paper, and are stencilled with a trellis pattern over which a cascade of rose petals seems to fall in an apparently random arrangement. The woodwork is black and the furniture is assembled from earlier commissions – the Argyle Street high back chairs and a sideboard converted from a cabinet he designed for his bedroom in the mid-1890s.

Mackintosh retained the original staircase and baluster but on the first-floor landing he removed one door, enlarged the window and made entry to the first-floor apartment through the original rear room, now converted to a studio for Margaret. The lower part of the wall between the original two rooms was removed to create one large L-shaped space. On the south wall Mackintosh blocked up the existing window and created a new, wide casemented window the proportions of which were more in keeping with Mackintosh's other changes to the room. He reduced the visual height of the room by introducing a wall plate which encircled it, crossing the bay window of the east elevation. He built a false wall above this plate, thus hiding the full height of the bay window and that adjacent to it. This wall plate continued at the same height in the studio, linking door and fireplace; on the west wall he did not close off the window but simply ran the plate across it and pierced it to emphasise its function. None of the furniture seems to have been designed specifically for his new house. Much of it was made for Mains Street in 1900 but there are also some later pieces, including items made for the Turin exhibition of 1902.

On the second floor Mackintosh combined two rooms again to provide a larger L-shaped bedroom where he used the white painted furniture designed for his Mains Street apartment in 1900.

Behind and above the bedroom, in a new space not present in the original house, is a gallery displaying items from the large collection of Mackintosh's work held by the University, including the guest bedroom suite of furniture from 78 Derngate, Northampton.

Mackintosh in Glasgow

Lady Artists' Club

1908 • Charles Rennie Mackintosh
5 Blythswood Square, Glasgow G2 4AD

55.863891, -4.2627275
NS 58488 65749
Private

Subway: Cowcaddens
Bus: First Bus 9, 11, 20, 44, 44A, 57,
57A
North side of Blythswood Square

Mackintosh added this faux-classical door, behind which was a panelled entrance hall and telephone box formed out of intersecting grids, forerunners of the Chinese Room and Derngate interiors. Mackintosh is in games-playing mode with his tongue-in-cheek references to classical motifs and fluted columns similar to those in the Board Room at the School of Art. In 1896–8 George Walton had provided the Lady Artists with a gallery in the basement that included a grand fireplace in stone and wrought iron.

House for Dr Calderwood, Barrhead

1898 • Charles Rennie Mackintosh
5 Arthurlie Avenue, Barrhead G78 2BT

55.797855, -4.3908576
NS 50220 58650
Private

Rail: Barrhead
From Main Street (A736) take Ralston Road, then first left on to Arthurlie Avenue.

A development of the design for Redlands (pages 84–5) with a more confident handling of massing and detail. The cylindrical tower is much more dominant here than at Redlands and its unmodelled ashlar points to Mackintosh's involvement. As at Redlands, many of the interior features show a diluted Glasgow Style with Mackintosh, or his office colleagues, presumably working within the constraints imposed either by the client or the practice partners.

Wrought-iron Lamp at
Skelmorlie and Wemyss Bay Parish Church

c.1894 • Charles Rennie Mackintosh
Shore Road, Skelmorlie PA17 5DY
Skelmorlie and Wemyss Bay Parish Church, Church of Scotland

55.8724, -4.8900
NS 19286 68130
Open
01475 520703

Rail: Wemyss Bay. The church is south
of the village centre on Shore Road.
The lamp is outside the church and
accessible at all times.

John Honeyman designed
the adjacent church in 1893
and Mackintosh may have
been involved in the office.
His authorship of the lamp
is suggested by an almost
identical lamp that appears
in Mackintosh's perspective
drawing for Martyrs' School
(pages 22–5).

Pulpit and Choir Stalls at Gourock Parish Church

1899 • Charles Rennie Mackintosh
41 Royal Street, Gourock PA19 1PW
Old Gourock and Ashton Parish Church, Church of Scotland

55.958342, -4.815888
NS 24280 77522
Private
01475 659276

Rail: Gourock
Ferry: Caledonian McBrayne
  and Gourock/Kilcreggan/
  Helensburgh ferry
At junction of Binnie Street
  and Royal Street, Gourock

There is very little evidence remaining of Honeyman & Keppie's work here in 1899–1900 apart from some pieces of church furniture – a pulpit and choir stalls *in situ* and a communion table now at Penpont Church, Dumfriesshire. The furniture betrays Mackintosh's involvement but little of the other work completed (a substantial £2,500 worth of it) is recognisable (or survives) today.

Kilmacolm and Bridge of Weir

The arrival of the railway transformed these two Renfrewshire villages into dormitory communities for Paisley, Greenock and Glasgow. The eastern approach to Kilmacolm, in particular, festooned with grand new houses, became a showcase for Glasgow architects vying with each other for a share of this new work. Mackintosh had two clients here, William Davidson (Windyhill) and H.B. Collins (Auchenbothie etc.). Honeyman & Keppie also designed a house for Bernard Doulton in Kilmacolm and had at least one client in Bridge of Weir. Mackintosh might have been expected to gain more commissions here, but it was not to be. Visitors to Kilmacolm should look out for other 'modern' houses, such as James Salmon (Junior)'s own house, Rowantreehill, near Mackintosh's Windyhill.

Mackintosh outside Glasgow

Redlands (now Beauly), Bridge of Weir

1898–9 • Charles Rennie Mackintosh
Hazelwood Road, Bridge of Weir PA11 3DW

55.850786, -4.5763477
NS 38814 64956
Private

On foot, from the centre of the
village take Prieston Road (south-
west) and then turn left on
Hazelwood Road; Beauly is at the
corner of Hazelwood Road and
Kilgraston Road

One of a group of substantial Renfrewshire houses that may well have
been Keppie commissions. None of them has any specific Mackintosh
connection, but a certain wayward individuality suggests that someone
other than the more prosaic Keppie was involved in their design. In
the later 1890s that could only have been Mackintosh. At Redlands
the attached cylindrical tower at the right of the entrance elevation
speaks of Mackintosh and a similar feature appears at Dr Calderwood's
house (page 80). Internally, some generic Glasgow Style fittings show
Mackintosh's influence among his draughtsman colleagues at Honeyman
& Keppie, if not actually his own hand.

Mackintosh outside Glasgow

Gravestone for James Reid, Kilmacolm

1898 • Charles Rennie Mackintosh
Kilmacolm Cemetery, Port Glasgow Road, Kilmacolm PA13 4SF
Inverclyde Council

55.899932, -4.637947
NS 35432 70753
Open September–March, 8am–5pm;
   April–August, 8am–9pm.

Leave Kilmacolm on A761, Port Glasgow Road, towards Port Glasgow; on right about 800m after Wateryetts Drive, lane entrance via sharp right-hand turn

James Reid was the father-in-law of William Davidson, an early client and supporter of Mackintosh who commissioned Windyhill from him in 1899.

Although probably owing something to traditional gravestones that Mackintosh had sketched on his English holidays in the mid-1890s, the vocabulary of this memorial is pure Spook School.

As an architect Mackintosh was able to use this highly personal vocabulary on a much larger scale than his friends Herbert MacNair and the Macdonald sisters who, with the exception of posters and the occasional wall decoration, were generally limited to the design of domestic metalwork and watercolours. Mackintosh used such imagery in many of his projects in the 1890s but rarely offered any Rosetta stone to interpret the imagery. This gravestone, however, was illustrated as an accompaniment to a letter in the *British Architect* in 1912, in which the writer, almost certainly Mackintosh, regretted the paucity of design for modern gravestones. The *British Architect* describes the two figures flanking the stone as 'two angels in low relief guarding the grave [taking] the form of the poppy "the emblem of sleep"'. Would that Mackintosh had offered more such explanations and thus save us from some of the more extreme interpretations of his imagery.

Mackintosh outside Glasgow

Windyhill, Kilmacolm

1900–1 • Charles Rennie Mackintosh
Rowantreehill Road, Kilmacolm PA13 4NR

55.889513, -4.619901
NS 36222 69431
Private

From Bridge of Weir, take the A761 to
Kilmacolm; after entering the village
take second right, Porterfield Road,
and then second left. Windyhill is
200m on left.

Mackintosh's first house on a hill, commissioned by William Davidson, who had been an early client of the young Mackintosh in the mid-1890s, and who was to remain a friend and supporter for the rest of his life, and beyond.

The house looks south and presents a severe face to the prevailing wind and rain – and sometimes the sun. The plan is L-shaped, with the service wing running off to the north and north-east and an entrance almost hidden in the north elevation, seemingly part of

Mackintosh outside Glasgow

the apsidal staircase. The house is harled and has barely any of the sculptural decoration or even dressed stone to be found on earlier, or contemporary, Mackintosh designs. In a way, the exterior is all about the roofscape, with dramatic expanses of slates to north and south, which cascade around chimneys in the service wing. Windows are treated variously and are often just punched into the harled walls in an asymmetric composition. Only in the southern bay window and the northern dormer does this vary to any extent.

Inside, the main rooms are arranged along an axial east–west plan and face south over the steeply sloping garden. The hall and staircase connect them and each is an important element in the overall composition. Mackintosh furnished several rooms in the house and these items are now in the collection of the Glasgow School of Art.

Windyhill is a hillside castle, whose exterior belies its internal comfort. It is understated and, at first glance, even simplistic, but its integrity and elegance outclass all of its *fin-de-siècle* neighbours in Kilmacolm.

Mackintosh outside Glasgow

Gate Lodge, Auchenbothie, Kilmacolm

1901–2 • Charles Rennie Mackintosh
Port Glasgow Road, Kilmacolm PA13 4SF

55.899932, -4.637947
NS 35180 70577
Private

Leave Kilmacolm on the A761, Port
Glasgow Road, towards Port
Glasgow; lodge on right about
800m after Wateryetts Drive, at
junction with lane to cemetery

A simple cottage, commissioned by H.B. Collins, who was to give Mackintosh several future commissions in Kilmacolm. A pyramidal roof with central chimney sits above a plainly Voyseyesque design with the most noteworthy feature being the sloping buttress in the middle of the entrance elevation. The plan is very straightforward with four rooms grouped around a central fireplace block.

Cloak, Kilmacolm

1906–15 • Charles Rennie Mackintosh
Cloak Road, Kilmacolm PA13 4SD

55.912301, -4.637073
NS 35297 71974
Private

From Kilmacolm take either High
Street and Finlayston Road for
1 mile to Cloak Road, or Port
Glasgow Road for 2 miles to Cloak
Road; house equidistant from
either junction

Variously known as Mossyde, Balgray Cottage, Mosside, Cloak Cottage and Ploughman's Cottage, this project has caused confusion for many years. H.B. Collins first commissioned a small cottage at Cloak in 1906 and over most of the next decade commissioned Mackintosh to extend it on at least three occasions. The west wing of the house comprises the original cottage, identified through its thick rubble walls and deep splayed windows. In 1908 Mackintosh was asked to extend the cottage to the south and west, which was done relatively seamlessly. In fact Mackintosh seems to have been intent on implying a natural organic growth in the building – it is his most vernacular design – with an emphasis on rubble masonry, albeit with dressed corners. The final phase, slightly more confused in its chronology, extended the house north, creating a range of deeply set windows on the east front and a large battered chimneystack as its only articulation. Some original features survive inside, but the house was always firmly rooted in cottage architecture, despite its growing size, and other than a few fireplaces there is little there to identify the house as a Mackintosh design.

Auchenbothie Mains, Kilmacolm

1913–14 • Charles Rennie Mackintosh
Netherwood Road, Kilmacolm PA13 4SH

55.901296, -4.651164
NS 34348 70751
Private

From Kilmacolm take Port Glasgow Road (A761) past Auchenbothie Gate Lodge. After 500m take the road to left and then left again over a disused railway line. Auchenbothie Mains is 200m to the south-west.

Another, minor, commission from H.B. Collins. Mackintosh provided a small extension to the existing farmhouse (not visible from the road) and a porch (now enclosed) with bathroom above. The drawings at The Hunterian show a rather more elaborate project than that finally executed.

Helensburgh

A single pier serving river traffic linked the burgh of Helensburgh to Glasgow, Greenock and Paisley from the beginning of the nineteenth century. It was already fashionable as a bathing town long before the arrival of the railway in 1857, but it then became a thriving dormitory for Glasgow businessmen, growing rapidly along its extended grid plan. In 1894 a second railway line (from Glasgow to Oban and Fort William) provided a station nearer the top of the hill overlooking the town and the Clyde and generated a second building boom, the northern boundary of which was the plot bought by Walter Blackie for his new house commissioned from Mackintosh.

This house was in stark contrast to most of those around it, with the sole exception of Baillie Scott's White House, 15 Upper Colquhoun Street (1898). English Arts and Crafts (and Norman Shaw) was the predominant style for houses in Upper Helensburgh, the best of them by A.N. Paterson and William Leiper. As at Kilmacolm, Mackintosh failed to win any more domestic commissions but the town is left with his most complete and successful house – The Hill House.

HELENSBURGH.

Helensburgh and Gareloch Conservative Club

1894–5 • Charles Rennie Mackintosh
40 Sinclair Street, Helensburgh G84 7QE

56.003747, -4.733458
NS 29673 82333
Private

Rail: Helensburgh Central from Queen
  Street Low Level
Leave station via Princes Street East
  entrance, turn right and left at
  junction with Sinclair Street

The clue to the true authorship of this building is in the details and the wilful oddity of the street elevation. Honeyman & Keppie, probably riding on the success of their Glasgow Art Club, designed this club with two ground-floor shops (now lost to pretty awful modern replacements), a top-lit public hall and general club function rooms and an attic

top-lit billiards room. As at the Glasgow Art Club, Mackintosh seems to have had a considerable hand in the design, most notably in the Sinclair Street elevation. The left-hand half of this comprises a shallow bay with mullioned and transomed windows, articulated by bold mouldings, decorative scroll sculpture beneath the second-floor window and high-relief stylised tree set against the parapet of the building. On the right-hand half, the first floor window lies within the plane of the main wall but a bay appears above it, echoing the adjacent bay window to its left. The single window in the bay is supported on a scrolled cushion and the shafts either side of it, like those in the wider bay, rise out of carved heads and terminate in naturalistic foliage capitals. Between these two bays a niche containing a sculpture of St Andrew is placed rather oddly, with his feet at the transom height of the flanking windows but otherwise the niche does not correspond in its placement to any other nearby feature. If all this were not enough to confirm Mackintosh's involvement, then at the centre of the parapet is a section of pierced tracery, surely a reworking of a drawing in one of Mackintosh's sketchbooks of his travels in southern England. In some ways this obscure and little-known building shows the developing Mackintosh in a better light than the Herald, Queen Margaret College or Martyrs' School. His commitment to architectural sculpture and ornament is here confirmed, and makes the authorship of the Renfrew Street elevation of the School of Art, apart from its entrance, more questionable.

Mackintosh outside Glasgow

The Hill House, Helensburgh

1902–4 • Charles Rennie Mackintosh
4 Upper Colquhoun Street, Helensburgh G84 9AJ
The National Trust for Scotland

56.017210, -4.728724
NS 30008 83831
Open 1 April–31 October, daily 1.30–
   5.30pm. For admission charges visit
   www.nts.org.uk/Property/The-Hill-
   House/Prices/
0844 493 8808

Rail: Helensburgh Central. Trains from
   Glasgow Queen Street Lower level
   (half-hourly service, journey takes
   50 minutes) and then a 1½ mile
   half walk uphill on Sinclair Street,
   or a short taxi ride from outside
   the station. Less frequent trains also
   run from Glasgow Queen Street to
   Upper Helensburgh Station, which
   is much closer to the house.
Off A818, between A82 and A814, 23
   miles north-west of Glasgow.

Mary Newbery Sturrock, a good friend of the Mackintoshes and daughter of Francis Newbery, once said that she had longed to see Mackintosh's fiftieth house. Sadly, it was not to be and by default The Hill House, only his second completed house, became his domestic masterpiece.

Although sharing many similarities with Windyhill in Kilmacolm, it is a much grander house, more thoughtfully planned, and decorated internally to suit the social standing of one of Scotland's most influential publishers. It follows Windyhill's L-plan, with an east–west axis for the main rooms and a service wing running north from the east edge of the garden elevation. The house is fully harled, like Windyhill, but its massing is much more skilful with an interplay of roofs, staircase towers, walls, chimneys and window bays manipulating light and shade to create an ever-changing pattern. Mackintosh had also intended, judging by his early perspective drawings of the house, to incorporate some carved decoration here, but the finished building excludes it except for the nominal appearance of dressed stone details and door casings. Whether it was the victim of Blackie's cost-cutting or a change of heart in its architect is not known.

The house is entered on the west side, an elevation diminished by the final exclusion of the billiards room originally planned to the north of the main door. All the same, it is a fine abstract composition, setting the standard for further such detailing around the upper part of the dining room gable to the east.

The garden front, looking south, shows Mackintosh playing games: at its west edge the library window is set deep within the thickness of the wall while the tiny bedroom window above it is punched through a shallow bay. The vestiges of Mackintosh's plan to place carvings either side of this window can still be seen in the harled 'shutters' flanking the window. The harling flows over them just as it does the wall heads of the building; none of the traditional stone or tiled finishes is used here, or around the chimneys, which adds to the monolithic feel of the structure but also has caused underlying structural problems due to penetration of water. The fenestration of library, drawing room, bedrooms above and window bay differs constantly, bringing agility to what could otherwise be a rather gaunt elevation, as it is at Windyhill. The window bay looks almost insubstantial compared to the mass of the rest of the house, but inside its true nature is revealed and it is fully integrated with the internal arrangement and decoration.

To the east the dining room gable projects, with changing window patterns again and a fine arrangement of chimneys and receding wall planes at its top. The house turns the corner to the north rather uncertainly and the service wing is melded to it with a turret staircase, again with an apparently haphazard arrangement of windows. The lower level of the east elevation is obscured by ancillary structures but the first floor is dominated by the shallow bay window at the left, south, edge and by the glazed pavilion of the children's playroom on the floor above.

The north elevation, with a subsidiary entrance direct into the hall for visitors for the family rather than for Mr Blackie (whose office-cum-library was placed at the side of the west entrance), is cluttered by drainpipes and suffers from the removal of the billiards room, although the apsidal wall of the main staircase, as at Windyhill, makes a strong statement.

Entering the house through the west door, visitors are drawn through the dark vestibule towards the brightly lit hall. First, however, on the right, is the library, used by Mr Blackie for the occasional business visitor and out of the way of the general traffic of the house. You may hear it said that Mr Blackie specified that his library and the children's playroom should be as far apart as possible; it may be so but Mackintosh had already incorporated such a layout at the House for an Art Lover and it was not an unusual arrangement in houses of the period. The library is panelled in dark-stained wood, enlivened by such details as the miniature writing cabinet adjacent to the fireplace and pieces of coloured glass inset into the panelling. Moving east along the entrance axis, visitors for the family would advance out of the small, dark vestibule up four steps into the main hall, a bright room lit by the staircase windows and by its own windows which face on to the north courtyard. It is furnished as a reception room, with chairs and table, and a splendid fireplace and panelled walls as at Windyhill. Between the panelling, the walls are stencilled with an abstract pattern based on geometrical and organic motifs.

The main axis from the front door effectively ends in this hall, where doors lead off to the drawing room and dining room, for its continuation is only into the service quarters. Indeed, the axial direction which the visitor would take, enticed into the hall by its brighter lighting and strong colours, is broken as soon as he decides to leave the hall, for all the main rooms are placed at 90° to it. Even the staircase involves a 180° turn, but after another four steps one encounters a small ingle with a fitted seat, overlooking the hall fireplace through an open screen. To ascend further means turning through another 90° to a half landing, apsidal as at Windyhill, and turning again through 180° to the first-floor landing, where the bedroom corridor once again follows an east–west axis.

The drawing room to the south is a much smaller room than that provided for the House for an Art Lover but Mackintosh devised a plan

which similarly gives the drawing room various quite separate functions. Directly opposite the door from the hall is a wide window seat, flanked by fitted book and magazine racks, contained in a bay with a lower ceiling than the rest of the room; outside, the bay is expressed as a stark, glazed projection from the main elevation of the house. With a wide view over Helensburgh and the Clyde, this was effectively a summer room, with central heating under the seat to provide some warmth when the weather was cool. In winter, domestic life was concentrated around the fireplace on the wall opposite this bay window. With only a much smaller window to let in winter light from the south, this part of the room was warmer, and the furniture, particularly the large couch, was so arranged as to shut out the colder bay and any draughts from the hall. At the far end of the room was another bay, formed by a reduction in the height of the ceiling, in which was kept the grand piano. This large piece of furniture had its own carefully defined territory so that it did not encroach, spatially at least, upon the rest of the drawing room.

The floors of the two bays were bare wooden boards, but the main part of the drawing room, as defined by the full-height ceiling, was carpeted. The design was of squares laid out in a perimeter aisle, as in the hall carpet. In 1904 the lighting of the room was provided by four large glass and metal fittings, each combining the motifs of square and circle. There was no cornice between wall and ceiling, both of which were originally painted white; below the moulding that encircled the room at door and fireplace height, the walls were stencilled with a pattern of roses in green and pink, contained in a framework of stencilled silver panels with chequered decoration. In November 1905, quotations were obtained for wall lights to replace the four ceiling fittings; perhaps they did not provide enough illumination or possibly smoke from the gas jets was staining the ceiling. In 1912, Mackintosh's notebook (in the collections at The Hunterian) shows that he revisited The Hill House to advise on redecoration and the repair and recovering of some items of furniture. This is confirmed by the firm's job books. Mackintosh's notes quite clearly state that the drawing-room ceiling was to be painted 'plum', and one of Blackie's daughters remembers it having a warmer tone than pure black. It has been suggested that this step was taken because of the dirty marks which were continually made on the frieze by the gas wall lamps, but these can have been no worse than similar marks in rooms elsewhere in the house where ceilings were not painted a dark colour. A more likely reason for the new colour scheme was to redress the balance between the ceiling and the rest of the room after it was upset by the removal of the four large light fittings. These had been fixed to the ceiling, and their lower edges were level with the tops of the doors and the fireplace. They provided a continuation of this specific level, about 2.4m above the floor, especially when they were lit: as the gas jets were in the lower part of the fitting, they would have distracted attention from the ceiling. When they were replaced by wall lamps, the ceiling was left bare, and this large unbroken plane became much more dominant in the composition of the room than had been intended. By darkening it, Mackintosh attempted to reduce the reflectiveness of the ceiling and thus distract from its impact on the rest of the room.

In the dining room, as with all of Mackintosh's earlier domestic dining-rooms, the emphasis is upon dark walls, a pale ceiling, and concentrated pools of light over the table and around the fireplace. A simple grate on the south wall is flanked by two large escutcheons of polished steel which hold the fire irons; above these an expanse of plaster inset with groups of four tiles obviate the need for an overmantel. Illumination is provided by two elaborate wall lights (which are duplicated on the north wall) and a single light fitting suspended over the dining table.

The first-floor corridor, like that at Windyhill, contains linen cupboards and a fitted alcove seat looking out to the north. The corridor repeats the east–west axis of the entrance hall, with the bedrooms similarly ranged off to the south. Most of the rooms have no fittings other than very simple fireplaces, with small panels of stencil decoration on the walls. Apart from the main bedroom and Mr Blackie's dressing room, the only room of interest on the first floor is the day nursery and on the second floor, the playroom. In the day nursery, which faces east, a full-height bow window echoes that of the breakfast room, similarly positioned, in the House for an Art Lover designs. The playroom also refers to the competition design, with its polygonal bay window looking out over the service wing and the garden.

Mr and Mrs Blackie's bedroom, like the main bedroom in the House for an Art Lover, is placed at the end of the corridor, out of the way of all the other bedrooms and well away from the children's rooms. A dressing room for Mr Blackie is attached. Mackintosh has attempted to define the different functions the main bedroom had to fulfil. As one enters, the room appears rectangular with a flat ceiling; to the left is the fireplace and, at 90° to it, a wall of fitted furniture – settle and wardrobes. In fact, the room is L-shaped, and in the large area to the west are the bed and more fitted wardrobes. This sleeping alcove is defined by a vaulted ceiling, the curve of the vault echoed by a concave bay in the south wall through which a small window admits daylight to the bed. In his original drawing, Mackintosh shows a screen of glass and timber with curtains at the junction of the vault with the flat ceiling, which effectively partitions the bed from the more public part of the room with its fireplace and couch. This feature was never executed. The lower parts of the walls were decorated with a stencil based on a trellis intertwined with briar roses. Mackintosh continued to provide furniture for the house long after it was completed – the elaborate desk in the drawing room, a clock, easy chairs and garden furniture.

The Hill House had only one private owner after the Blackies left, Mr and Mrs Tom Campbell Lawson. As a governor of Glasgow School of Art, Campbell Lawson had access to the necessary expertise to preserve the house more or less as Mackintosh had left it. In the early 1970s he sought a public owner for the house, offering it on very generous terms, but it was not a period when such acquisitions were easy for local authorities or universities. Eventually, the Royal Incorporation of Architects in Scotland stepped into the breach, in a bold move that extended their role into that of museum or historic house proprietor. To help finance the venture, the east wing was divided horizontally into three apartments, one on each floor. The top floor, containing the day nursery, was acquired by the Landmark Trust, and is still available for short-term rental (2011). The remaining apartments were restored to the house after 1982 when The Hill House was donated to the National Trust for Scotland with the aid of an endowment from the National Heritage Memorial Fund.

Mackintosh outside Glasgow

Interiors at Dunglass Castle, Bowling (removed)

1900 • Charles Rennie Mackintosh
Dumbarton Road, Bowling G60 5BP

55.929390, -4.5026806
NS 43741 73532
Private

Entrance to site on Dumbarton
Road, east of Dunglass roundabout
(junction of A814 and A82). Access
restricted but house visible from river,
passing trains and nearby cycle path.

The Macdonald family moved into Dunglass Castle after Talwin Morris left to go up the hill to Torwood, overlooking the Clyde. Frances and Margaret Macdonald, Mackintosh and Herbert MacNair all made some contribution to the new decorations for Dunglass. Mackintosh designed furniture for the bedrooms, some of it now lost, and made alterations to the library, including the fireplace and a settle incorporating decorative fabrics by the sisters.

About 1960 the various items designed by The Four were removed from the castle and several were given to the Royal Scottish Museum and the University of Glasgow, where they are periodically on display. The castle is now derelict, hidden inside the compound of the now unused oil terminal, which bought it in the 1930s.

Wall Stencils at St Serf's Church, Dysart

1901 • Charles Rennie Mackintosh
West Port, Dysart, Kirkcaldy KY1 2TD
Dysart Parish Church, Church of Scotland

56.125893, -3.1246233
NT 30186 93143
Open by appointment, telephone 01592 651293

The connection between Mackintosh or his firm and St Serf's (now the parish church) is unknown, but in 1901 he was commissioned to provide a series of stencilled decorations, now the largest surviving example of such work. A series of panels were incorporated around each of the two apsidal transepts, using favourite motifs – a dove of peace and the Tree of Knowledge. The panels were painted over in the 1920s and are now being restored to view in an ongoing conservation project.

Brough & Macpherson, Comrie

1903–4 • Charles Rennie Mackintosh
1 Dunira Street, Comrie PH6 2DN
The Landmark Trust

56.374228, -3.987831
NN 77312 21995
Private

A85 Comrie, corner of Dunira Street
and Melville Square

How this job came to Honeyman Keppie & Mackintosh is not known but it was commissioned by a local draper and ironmonger, Peter Macpherson, as a shop with a flat above and workrooms in the attics. Mackintosh, judging by entries in his firm's job-books, certainly had control of the project but the design can not be said to be overwhelmingly typical. The only feature vaguely suggestive of his hand is the oddly placed attached turret with conical roof which projects at first floor level on the corner of the building.

The flat above is now available to rent from the Landmark Trust, which also has an apartment in the service wing at The Hill House, Helensburgh.

Chancel Furniture at Holy Trinity Church, Bridge of Allan

1904 • Charles Rennie Mackintosh
12 Keir Street, Bridge of Allan FK9 4NW
Holy Trinity Church, Church of Scotland

56.153420, -3.9471120
NS 79145 97345
Open on Saturdays, June, July
   and August 10am–4pm; or by
   arrangement
01786 834155 or 01786 832093

Rail: Bridge of Allan
Several bus routes from Stirling
From railway station take Henderson
   Street (A9) south-east, turn right
   on to Fountain Road to junction
   with Keir Street

The most elaborate of all Mackintosh's designs for church furnishings, extending to pulpit, organ screen, communion table and chairs. The design is a development of the communion table at Queen's Cross Church with elements of the Board Room at Glasgow School of Art.

Gravestone for Orrock Johnstone

1905 • Charles Rennie Mackintosh
Wemyss and MacDuff Cemetery, Main Road, East Wemyss KY1 4RH
Fife Council

56.162144, -3.0618864
NT 34148 97116
Open 9am until dusk

From cemetery gates follow tarmac path to right until it begins to loop to the left; the gravestone is on the right, in the corner near the boundary walls

Johnstone, a native of East Wemyss, had been minister at Westbourne Free Church, Glasgow, which had commissioned the mission halls at Ruchill (page 52). One of Mackintosh's hovering birds spreads its wings over the inscription and they seem to be extended metaphorically into the oval of the main part of the design. The inscription was originally made direct into the sandstone by McGilvray & Ferris but because of continuing erosion has now been covered by a replica in copper.

Gravestone for Talwin Morris, Dumbarton

1911 • Charles Rennie Mackintosh
Stirling Road, Dumbarton G82 2JD
West Dunbartonshire Council

55.949704, -4.5495093
NS 40900 75899
Open Monday–Saturday, 8.30am until
dusk but no later than 8pm; Sunday
and public holidays, 9am until dusk
but no later than 7pm

Rail: Dumbarton East or Dumbarton
Central
At the intersection of Stirling Road
(A82) and Garshake Road,
Dumbarton
From the entrance to the cemetery
take path to left and then second
right

A very simple, proto-Art Deco design. Morris had been Art Director
for the Blackie publishing house and had introduced Mackintosh to
Walter Blackie when he was looking for an architect for a new house at
Helensburgh (pages 98–105).

Auchenibert, Killearn

1905–8 • Charles Rennie Mackintosh
Ibert Road, Killearn G63 9PY

56.042478, -4.36007
NS 53084 85780
Private

From Main Street follow Ibert Road
then second lane on left

The last of Mackintosh's major domestic commissions in Scotland. Its Tudorbethan style was apparently requested by the client, F.J. Shand, with whom Mackintosh did not get on well. There are few, if any, of the usual Mackintosh flourishes; even the published perspective was drawn by one of his assistants, Graham Henderson. Inside, a few details suggest more of Mackintosh's hand than are apparent in the external masonry – fireplaces, casement details, some panelling – but it was not his finest hour. A.D. Hislop was called in to complete the job after Mackintosh and the Shands parted company.

78 Derngate, Northampton

1916–17 • Charles Rennie Mackintosh
78 Derngate (enter via 82 Derngate), Northampton NN1 1UH
78 Derngate Northampton Trust

52.235514, -0.889893
SP 75913 60289
Open February–December,
Tuesday–Sunday, 10am–5pm;
telephone 01604 603 407 or see
www.78derngate.org.uk for details.
Visit by guided tour. Entrance fee.

Rail: Northampton Station. Follow
signs for Town Centre and 78
Derngate; 10–25 mins walk.
Bus: Northampton Bus Station

The most complete of Mackintosh's various commissions in England.
The house was bought as a wedding present by his parents for
W.J. Bassett-Lowke and his bride, Florence Jones. Bassett-Lowke asked
Mackintosh to make substantial alterations to the house, including new
furniture which was made by German craftsmen interned on the Isle
of Man.

Mackintosh outside Glasgow

The front door gives an immediate insight of what is to come – Mackintosh anticipating Art Deco by a decade. Much of the inspiration for the interiors here came from Mackintosh's knowledge of what was happening in Vienna but this by no means diminishes his achievement. The house consists of three floors plus a basement and Mackintosh made the most sweeping change to its plan by turning the staircase through 90° to run across the house rather than straight from the front door. On the ground floor this created two apartments, a hall-parlour and a dining room that were the focus of Mackintosh's work in the house. The hall-parlour is predominantly black, with a stencilled pattern of stylised trees providing intense colour to relieve the overall darkness of the room. The furniture was also painted black, but was relieved by mirror glass and coloured insets of plastic. The staircase screen, also black with a partly-white newel post, interweaves an abstract pattern of leaded and mirror glass and plastic inlay in its overall trellis construction. Squares and triangles dominate the composition here – organic decoration gives way to geometric stylisation of natural forms.

The dining room is a much calmer space, dominated by a bank of cabinets and fireplace and extended by a loggia overlooking the garden. This loggia takes a different form on each of the upper floors and transforms the garden elevation of the house into a proto-International Style composition.

The top floor is devoted to a guest bedroom, effectively the last room complete with furniture that Mackintosh was to design and one of his most accomplished. The original furniture is now at The Hunterian in Glasgow but an excellent replica helps capture the intensity of the space.

78 Derngate has had a chequered past since the Bassett-Lowkes left it in the early 1920s but in recent years it has been the subject of a careful restoration which has won many awards and sets the bar high for other owners of Mackintosh buildings whose properties are in need of care and attention.

The Drive, Northampton

1919 • Charles Rennie Mackintosh
5 The Drive, Northampton NN1 4RZ

52.250391, -0.87816183
SP 76682 61950
Private

Mackintosh provided furniture and a decorative scheme for a dining room here for F. Jones, brother-in-law of W.J. Bassett-Lowke, the owner of 78 Derngate. Some furniture remains but the stencilling has gone.

Bassett-Lowke had commissioned a similar scheme and furniture for his weekend retreat, Candida Cottage, Roade, Northants. Nothing is left of the Mackintosh designs here although the furniture mainly survives in private collections. Bedrooms which Mackintosh created for other friends of Bassett-Lowke, in Bath and elsewhere, have also been dismantled and the furniture scattered; one complete bedroom suite from this group is owned by the Victoria & Albert Museum, London.

49 Glebe Place, Chelsea

1919–21 • Charles Rennie Mackintosh
49 Glebe Place, London SW3 5JE

51.485228, -0.16999480
TQ 27162 77840
Private

Underground: Sloane Square
Bus: 11, 19, 22, 49, 211, 319
From Sloane Square take King's Road
to Glebe Place; 49 is on the south
side of the street

The only one of three adjacent studios designed for 48–50 Glebe Place to come to fruition – of a sort. Derwent Wood, Harold Squire and Arthur Blunt all asked Mackintosh to design studio-houses on the south side of Glebe Place in 1920. Several redesigns later, only Squire's house went forward, and that to a much reduced and disappointing design. Mackintosh's original plans for these studios and for the block of studio flats proposed for the ground south of them could have given new life to his architectural career in London, but it was not to be.

Mackintosh outside Glasgow

Little Hedgecourt, East Grinstead

1919 • Charles Rennie Mackintosh
Copthorne Road, Felbridge, East Grinstead RH19 2QQ

51.142098, -0.061336756
TQ 35714 39879
Private

Off Copthorne Road (A264) west
of junction with Mill Lane and
Rowplatt Lane

Mackintosh's client here was E.O. Hoppé, the photographer, whom he had met through friends in Chelsea after he moved there in 1915. Hoppé bought the house in 1915 and Mackintosh supervised a small addition and some internal alterations, including an ingle nook. Further extensions were planned, as well as a rather grand pigeon house, but the Hoppés sold the house before they could be carried out. The next owner, André Simon, made further alterations to the house which obscure Mackintosh's 1919 extension.

Boho (formerly The Roost), Glasgow

1900 • Clarke & Bell
53–61 Dumbarton Road, Glasgow G11 6NX

55.870003, -4.296378
NS 56307 66483
Open

Subway: Kelvin Hall
Bus: 11, 18, 23, 42, 44, 51, 57, 59

Much altered and now painted an unsympathetic black, this pub was a triumph of Art Nouveau lettering and florid woodwork, much of which is now obscured under new fascias and layers of paint.

11 Whittinghame Drive, Glasgow

1907 • John Ednie
11 Whittinghame Drive, Glasgow G12 0XS

55.884919, -4.315428
NS 55290 68166
Private

Rail: Anniesland
Bus: First Bus 20, 66, 92, 118
Great Western Road at Whittinghame
Drive

Known as much for his furniture and interiors as his architecture Ednie's best-known building is this fine Arts and Crafts villa in Glasgow's west end. Crowstep gables and corbelled bays give the silhouette drama but its originality is the interior with fine panelling and plasterwork and stained glass by Oscar Paterson.

Mackintosh's Contemporaries

12 University Gardens, Glasgow

1900 • J. Gaff Gillespie
12 University Gardens, Glasgow G12 8QQ
University of Glasgow

55.873294, -4.291092
NS 56779 66821
Private

Subway: Hillhead
Bus: First Bus 44, 44A, from the city
  centre to University Avenue
Parking: Metered
Off University Avenue at junction of
  Hillhead Street

The glory of this house is its interior, not officially open to the public, but it is where Gillespie shows his strength as a Glasgow Style designer. Although the overall mood is sombre, perhaps reflecting the presbyterian nature of the rest of this Burnet-designed terrace, the placing of detail is handled with aplomb reflecting what Gillespie had learned from Mackintosh. Stained glass by Oscar Paterson and much internal carving make this one of the finest Glasgow Style interiors of its era. Outside Gillespie has on the whole adhered to Burnet's adjacent examples but the baroque doorcase and octagonal tower contained within the façade show that he is only ever his own man.

Gravestone for the MacNair Family, Largs

c.1900 • James Herbert MacNair
Largs Cemetery, Dalry Road (Hailey Brae), Largs KA30 9PR
North Ayrshire Council

55.784543, 4.8551470
NS 21062 58272
Open
01475 673149

Rail: Largs
Bus: From Springfield gardens, 40, 45, 585, 585A, 800
From the cemetery gates take the tarmac drive to the left; continue past a drive entering from the left and the gravestone is on the right in the third row up the hill

A rather grand Glasgow Style headstone appropriate to the standing of the MacNairs, who at that time lived in a huge mansion overlooking Skelmorlie, to the north of Largs (although by 1910 the family was bankrupt). At its centre is the MacNair crest, a mermaid, which has sadly suffered from erosion in this exposed location.

McConnel's Building, Cowcaddens, Glasgow

1906–7 • John Keppie
307–333 Hope Street, Glasgow G2 3PA

55.866185, -4.25673
NS 58868 66014
Private

Subway: Cowcaddens
Bus: First Bus 8, C8 3, 20, 38, 38A, 40,
    40A, 61, 66
At north end of Hope Street,
    opposite the Theatre Royal, at
    Cowcaddens Road

John Keppie's grand Beaux Arts tenement for the City Improvement Trust. Mackintosh's involvement is not formally recorded but the entrance doorcases, the treatment of the stairs above and the lively roofline all seem to point to Keppie at least learning something from his junior partner. Keppie also controlled the Annan building at 513 Sauchiehall Street, which contains rather more obvious Glasgow Style features probably inserted by junior draughtsmen in the office.

Caledonian Mansions, Glasgow

1895–7 • James Miller
445–459 Great Western Road, Glasgow G12 8HH

55.875082, -4.280698
NS 57400 66987
Private

Subway: Kelvinbridge
Bus: 11, 20, 44, 44A, 66, 118
Junction of Great Western Road and
Otago Street

Built over the new Kelvinbridge railway station (now disused, across the Kelvin from Kelvinbridge subway station) this block of mansion flats with shops at ground level shows Miller in a fantasy Arts and Crafts manner. A building designed to be seen from all sides – and each of them tantalisingly different – it incorporates too many architectural motifs and flourishes to list. It seems to take some features from the Herald building and Mackintosh himself perhaps took ideas from here for Martyrs' School and other unrealised designs for central Glasgow.

St Andrew's East Church, Dennistoun, Glasgow

1904 • James Miller
681–685 Alexandra Parade, Glasgow G31 3LN
St Andrew's East Parish Church, Church of Scotland

55.86291, -4.208622
NS 61875 65530
Private, visit by arrangement
0141 554 3620

Rail: Alexandra Parade
Bus: 36, 38, 38A, 42
Alexandra Parade (A8) at junction of
Easter Craigs

Miller in a more traditional Arts and Crafts mode, inspired by fifteenth-
and sixteenth-century Gothic churches, with more than a nod to Scottish
tower houses in its 'west' elevation to Alexandra Parade. The square bell
turret over the entrance shows an awareness of Mackintosh in its
overhanging eaves and playful design. Probably the best of his churches
but with a curiously plain interior.

See also the adjacent hall by James Salmon (Junior) and J. Gaff Gillespie
(1898–9), in a simple late Gothic fashion with Glasgow Style decorative
carvings in its east and west bays and a rather superfluous cupola at east
edge of roof.

Gravestone for Sallie Gemmell Blackie

1910 • Talwin Morris
Glasgow Necropolis, 92 Cathedral Square, Glasgow G4 0U2
Glasgow City Council

55.865394, -4.237692
NS 60482 65549
Open
0141 287 3961

Rail: High Street
Bus: 11, 19, 31, 38, 38A, 42, 56, 56A
Enter either from Cathedral Square,
over bridge adjacent to south
side of Cathedral, or via entrance
at junction of Wishart Street and
John Knox Street. Epsilon Division,
eastern side.

Talwin Morris (1865–1911) was appointed in 1893 as the first Art Director of the publishing house of Blackie. He introduced an Art Nouveau vocabulary to much of their output over the next eighteen years and also advised the Blackie family on various matters of design, famously recommending Mackintosh to Walter Blackie, brother of J. Alexander Blackie whose family grave this is, as architect for his new house at Helensburgh, (pages 98–105) For a time Morris lived at Dunglass Castle (page 106) before the Macdonald family moved there. See the nearby Mackintosh tombstone for Alexander McCall (page 12).

AT REST
ROSALIE GEMMELL
WIFE OF
J. ALEXANDER BLACKIE
DIED JULY 200? MCMXX

ALEXANDER BLACKIE
PUBLISHER
DIED NOV XVIII MCMXXXI AGED LXXXII YEARS

Warehouse, Howard Street, Glasgow

1904 • J. Gibb Morton
118–120 Howard Street, Glasgow G1 4ER

55.855994, -4.252775
NS 59076 64810
Private

Subway: St Enoch
Bus: First Bus 9, 11, 18, 38, 38A, 41 54,
    57, 57A, 66
Howard Street at Fox Street.
    Approach on foot either from
    Clyde Street and Fox Street, or
    Howard Street from south-east
    corner of St Enoch Square.

A little-known and totally unloved building which shows how far other architects could take the Glasgow Style. The architect's perspective drawing betrays its own stylistic homage to Mackintosh and gives the best illustration of the individual details of the design – overhanging eaves, central turret and dome, and the mannered fourth floor windows. Sadly, the elegant shop windows of the ground floor, and even the salubrity of the street itself, are long gone.

The Griffin (formerly The King's Arms), Glasgow

1903 • William Reid
266 Bath Street, Glasgow G2 4JP

55.865294, -4.268017
NS 58175 65902
Open

Rail: Charing Cross
Subway: Cowcaddens
Bus: First Bus 11, 18, 23, 42, 44, 51, 57, 59

One of the few remaining Glasgow Style pubs in the city centre, designed to catch trade from the theatre across the road. Its glass is not original and the interior much altered, although a few features remain.

22 Park Circus, Glasgow

1872–4 & 1897–9 • James Salmon (Junior) & J. Gaff Gillespie
22 Park Circus, Glasgow G3 6BE
Glasgow City Council

55.869436, -4.279647
NS 57441 66342
Open by arrangement
0141 287 8350

Subway: Kelvinbridge
South-west quadrant of Park Circus.
From Woodlands Road take
Lynedoch Street or Woodlands
Gate to Lynedoch Place, then Park
Circus Place to Park Circus

Into this magnificent Park Circus interior, Salmon and Gillespie added a ballroom in 1897–9, quintessential Glasgow Art Nouveau, not Mackintosh-inspired but a contemporary response to the extravagant interiors designed by James Boucher in 1874. The carving is believed to be by Derwent Wood, for whom Mackintosh would design a studio in London, with assistance perhaps from Albert Hodge and Johan Keller.

Rowantreehill, Kilmacolm

1898 • James Salmon (Junior)
Rowantreehill Road, Kilmacolm PA13 4NR

55.890123, -4.62007
NS 36203 69489
Private

Adjacent to Windyhill, see page 88

Built as the Salmon family home, this glorious Arts and Crafts composition shows the other side of the Free Style coin from Mackintosh's adjacent Windyhill. Scottish and English antecedents are melded together to create a fractured skyline above boisterous elevations which seem to have a little of everything. The well-preserved interior shows Salmon in a more restrained Glasgow Style manner.

British Linen Bank, Govan, Glasgow

1899 • James Salmon (Junior) and J. Gaff Gillespie
816 Govan Road, Glasgow G51 3UW

55.863067, -4.311619
NS 55422 65762
Private

Subway: Govan
Bus: First Bus 23, 45, 45C, 88, 90
Corner of Govan Road and Water
Row (now Bank of Scotland)

Although its interior has gone this, remains a fine example of Glasgow Free Style, although not quite approaching the originality of the Anderston Savings Bank (pages 136–7). Working around the framework of a typical tenement of its day, Salmon and Gillespie introduced large expanses of plain masonry growing into chimney stacks, robust drip mouldings and string courses, a bold corner tower articulating the two elevations and broad projecting eaves, which all firmly identify this as a Glasgow Style building. The sculpture is by Derwent Wood and Johan Keller, who with Hodge were probably also responsible for the interiors at 22 Park Circus (page 132).

Mackintosh's Contemporaries

Anderston Savings Bank, Argyle Street, Glasgow

1899–1900 • James Salmon (Junior) & J. Gaff Gillespie
Sculpture by Albert Hodge
752–756 Argyle Street, Glasgow G3 8UN

55.861616, -4.274148
NS 57766 65520
Private

Bus: First Bus X9, 42, x54, 62,
From junction of Elderslie Street and
St Vincent Street turn south on
Elderslie Street to Argyle Street;
turn left, east, on Argyle Street

Now seen completely out of context following the demolition of its original neighbours, Salmon & Gillespie's bank and tenement block seems isolated and almost as unreal as a movie set. This was once a prominent corner site in a busy area of the city and the architects developed the success of their Govan Road bank (pages 134–5). The main entrance here is not on the corner but off-set to the west and contained by an elaborate arch supported on elegant carved capitals. A deep cornice separates the ground floor of the bank from the upper tenement floors but the articulation of the bay windows, pediments and chimneys all reflect the stature of the ground-floor tenant. Although the actual turning of the corner is achieved very simply at ground level, a grand corner turret rises from the middle of the storey, ornamented by carved panels and elaborate piers and capitals until it bursts out above the adjoining eaves into a fanfare of carved decoration. A superb building marooned by the idiosyncrasies (and idiocies) of 1960s planning.

Lion Chambers, Glasgow

1905 • James Salmon (Junior) & J. Gaff Gillespie
172 Hope Street, Glasgow G2 2TX

55.863563, -4.25757
NS 58826 65673
Private

Subway: Cowcaddens
Bus: First Bus 12, 19, 29, 38, 45, 45C,
    56, 138
172 Hope Street, Glasgow, on east
    side between Bath Street and West
    Regent Street

Glasgow's second reinforced concrete building (the first being the Sentinel Works in Polmadie), which takes advantage of the material's strength to soar eight stories on a very narrow and deep site. Originally occupied by a law firm with artists' studios on the top floor, the decorative panels and sculptures are also cast rather than carved. Gillespie probably supervised the design.

The Hatrack, St Vincent Street, Glasgow

1899–1902 • James Salmon (Junior)
142a–144 St Vincent Street, Glasgow G2 5LQ

55.861802, -4.25853
NS 58737 65498
Private

Rail: Central Station, Queen Street
    Station
Bus: First Bus 5, 9, 11, 12, 20, 38, 38A,
    40, 40A, 41, 44, 57, 57A
On north side of St Vincent Street
    near junction with Hope Street

With this building Salmon confirmed his reputation as the most exciting Glasgow Style designer after Mackintosh. The site is no bigger than a standard house plot but Salmon has provided ten floors of office accommodation in a design that retains and provokes interest from floor to floor. The stonework is cut back to a bare minimum to provide maximum light through the bay windows. Individual, and idiosyncratic, features abound, from the stained glass of the two cylindrical windows on the ground floor, the wrought iron and the decorative sculpture (perhaps by Derwent Wood) to the playful roofscape (with its ornate pinnacle from which the building got its nickname). Every floor is different but the differences are fluid and natural, unlaboured. One feels the architect could have gone on forever inventing new compositions for each new level.

79 West Regent Street, Glasgow

1903–4 • James Salmon (Junior)
79 West Regent Street, Glasgow G2 2AR

55.863187, -4.25791
NS 5877 6562
Private

Corner of Hope Street and West
Regent Street, Glasgow

James Salmon (Junior) added lead-covered bay windows and a hipped roof with dormers to a mid-nineteenth-century house. The decorative lead panels between the floors are fine examples of Salmon's Glasgow Style work.

Bibliography

The two most important guides to Glasgow's buildings are perhaps too big or too heavy to slip into the pocket but they are indispensable for those who wish to know more about the city's arictecture and the context in which Mackintosh and his contemporaries were working:

Andor Gomme & David Walker, *Architecture of Glasgow* (London, 1987; 2nd revised edition)
   The first, and still unsurpassed history and analysis of Glasgow's architectural heritage. The illustrations, all in black and white, are more powerful in the earlier, 1968, edition.
Elizabeth Williamson, Anne Riches & Malcolm Higgs, *Glasgow: The Buildings of Scotland* (New Haven and London, 2005).
   In typical Pevsnerian format, a thorough and classic guide to the city's buildings.

OTHER WORKS

Charles McKean, David Walker & Frank Walker, *Central Glasgow* (Edinburgh, 2008)
Sam Small, *Greater Glasgow* (Edinburgh, 2008)
David Stark, *Charles Rennie Mackintosh and Co. 1854–2004* (Catrine, 2004)
   A fascinating history of Honeyman & Keppie by one of its recent directors.
Frank Arneil Walker, *Argyll and Bute* (New Haven and London, 2005; revised edition)
   For Helensburgh buildings.
Frank Arneil Walker, *The South Clyde Estuary* (Edinburgh, 1986)
   For Bridge of Weir and Kilmacolm
Andrew McLaren Young & A.M. Doak, *Glasgow at a Glance: An Architectural Handbook* (Glasgow, 1965; revised edition 1983)
   The first concise guide to Glasgow's buildings and still the best pocket survey, if not least for showing what we have lost since the mid-1960s.

Bibliography

Index